BEAUTY FROM THE INSIDE OUT
A GUIDE FOR BLACK WOMEN

Also by La Verne Powlis:

THE BLACK WOMAN'S BEAUTY BOOK

Beauty from the Inside Out

A GUIDE FOR BLACK WOMEN

La Verne Powlis

Doubleday

NEW YORK

1988

Library of Congress Cataloging-in-Publication Data
Powlis, La Verne, 1947–
Beauty from the inside out.
1. Beauty, Personal.   2. Afro-American women—Health
and hygiene.   I. Title.
RA778.P8834   1988   646.7'042'08996073   87–9110
ISBN 0-385-23631-X

To my grandmother . . . my cheerleader.

ACKNOWLEDGMENTS

The research between these pages represents years of dedication and commitment from the dermatologists in the National Medical Association.

I offer a special thanks to John A. Kenney, Jr., M.D., professor of dermatology; Harold E. Pierce, M.D., assistant professor of dermatology and soft-tissue surgery; both at Howard University College of Medicine, Washington, D.C.

And a special thanks to these doctors at King-Drew Medical Center in Los Angeles: A. Paul Kelly, M.D., head of dermatology; William Daniel Keith, M.D., professor of dermatology; James William Hobbs, M.D., associate professor of dermatology; Pearl E. Grimes, M.D., assistant professor of dermatology.

Also, special thanks to dermatologists Darlene D. Sampson, M.D., diplomate of the American Board of Dermatology, Inglewood, California; Greta Clark, M.D., Berkeley, California.

For information on breast care, special appreciation to Claudia R. Baquet, M.D., M.P.H., minority field program director, National Cancer Institute; Dr. Alfred Haynes, dean of Drew Postgraduate Medical School; Melvin A. Silverstein, M.D., medical director, the Breast Center in Van Nuys, California; Meredith Sirmans, M.D., medical director, Medical Services for Women in New York City. And to *Essence* magazine for its excellent article "Saving Our Breasts," by Peggy Ann Taylor (June 1986), which prompted my research.

For insight into the emotions, special thanks to Alvin Poussaint, M.D., associate professor of psychiatry and associate dean of the Harvard Medical School; Constance Hammen, Ph.D., professor of psychology, UCLA; Rex Johnson, Ph.D., assistant professor of Christian Education, Biola University; Minnie Claiborne, Ph.D.; Napoleon Vaughn, Ph.D.; Craig K. Polite, Ph.D.

For nutrition and health information, special thanks to Tazewell Banks, M.D., professor of medicine at Howard University College of Medicine and director of the Central Heart Station, D.C. General Hospital; Arike Logan, M.D., member of the board of directors, King-Drew Medical Center; Judith S. Stern, Sc.D., professor of nutrition, University of California at Davis; Carmen H. Grange, M.D., on staff at St. Vincent's Hospital in New York City; Francis O'Neil, dietician at the Pritikin Health and Fitness Center in

Los Angeles; Dr. An Thanh, Los Angeles. Thanks also to Yvonne Swann, *Ebony* magazine, for sending me the stack of health articles, especially "How to Add Ten Years to Your Life" by Charles Whitaker (June 1986).

For information on pregnancy, special thanks to Vanessa A. Castine, M.D., diplomate of the American Board of Obstetrics and Gynecology; Malverse Martin, M.D., both in Los Angeles.

For information on cosmetic dentistry, special thanks to Jerry Albus, D.D.S.; Don Kobashigawa, D.D.S., Burbank, California.

Special appreciation and thanks to the women who shared their personal stories of challenge and triumph to encourage and inspire us: Juanda Green, Janice Darling, Carla Dunlap, Kattie Errisson, Karen L. Woods, Esq.

Special thanks to the hairstylists who shared their knowledge and information: John Atchison, whose styling expertise is represented throughout the photographs in this book, Bruce Clark, model Peggy Dillard, Sterfon Demmings, Pam Eatmon, Afua Asiedu, Sonia Bullock, Mae Elliott, Norma Harris, La Fay, André Weeks, Thaddeus Winston, Clifford Peterson.

Thanks to Patti LaBelle for her willingness to share her creative thoughts on hair with us.

For assistance with skin care, thanks to the Cal-A-Vie Spa in California; Lydia Safati, Sarkli/Repéchage Ltd., New York; Annette Green, Fragrance Foundation, New York; Skinn by Nathalie; and Vita Fields' Precious Nails, both in Los Angeles.

And special thanks for their interviews to fashion model Iman; singer and actress Olga Adderley; fitness trainer Lisa Kingston.

Special thanks and appreciation to photographer George Selman for his professionalism and quality work throughout this book.

To Kate Segal, for her assistance on the manuscript, a special thank-you.

And to Tim Tierney for his help in converting my dot matrix into letter-quality, thank you.

A very warm thank you to the models and other women who were photographed for this book: Karen Armstrong, Mrs. Thelma Bright, Ingra Engram, Sheila Frazier, Jean Johnson, Naima, Musanna Overr, Joyce Peters, Abigail Price, Beverly Swanson, Treva Wilson, and Mrs. Anna Velasquez.

And thanks to makeup artists Rudy Calvo and LaLette Littlejohn, who made them even more beautiful.

Thanks to Mrs. Christine W. Ford for allowing me to use the photograph of her daughter, my buddy, Vivian Ford, who beat me to heaven.

To my editors at Doubleday, Susan Schwartz and Elithea Whittaker, for their dedication and commitment to this book, a very sincere thank you.

CONTENTS

SKIN NEWS

MAKING UP

SPECIAL EFFECTS

A CLOSING NOTE

BEAUTY FROM THE INSIDE OUT
A GUIDE FOR BLACK WOMEN

INTRODUCTION

Let's turn beauty inside out!

Experts in the fields of nutrition, physical fitness, cosmetology and psychology stress that taking care of ourselves *inside* is imperative if we want to look beautiful *outside*. It's called the mind-body connection, or a holistic approach to beauty. Holistic means attending to the whole person—all of you—both inside and out.

For Black women, a personal commitment to take time out for *you* may mean reshuffling priorities. With our unique roles as homemaker, student, artist or career woman—and sometimes *all* of the above—our schedule is already packed! How can we maximize our energies to nurture ourselves when there are so many pressures and so little time?

The answer is this: we must recognize the need for *balance*. Specialists agree that we should not forget that taking care of ourselves is vital. In order to function at our optimum, we must eat correctly, exercise daily and flex our self-esteem regularly. Since we've so much to do, it's our only choice!

And we need to care for our hair and skin and learn proper makeup techniques with equal diligence. Because a woman who feels good about herself *inside* is the woman who makes certain she always looks her best *outside*.

That's what this book is all about. *Beauty from the Inside Out: A Guide for Black Women* is a comprehensive approach to beauty for *you*. It recognizes your unique challenges, your well-earned successes, and applauds you, the contemporary Black woman.

In addition to exploring updated, researched information from nutritionists, psychologists, dermatologists and hair and skin-care experts, I've interspersed personal testimonies from women with whom you can identify. Each had to jump an emotional hurdle in her will to survive. Whether her task was to schedule exercise time into her already demanding day, or to lose forty-plus pounds, or to pull herself out of a debilitating depression, or to learn how-to correctly apply makeup as a stamp of self-esteem, she won! And so can *you*.

After you read through the book once, there's an index to help you find specific subjects to refer to time and again. And a list of books I've found helpful during my years of research is referenced in the back.

It's all here, written to you from my heart. The outward expression of beauty comes from an inner experience. So between these pages you'll find the threads of inner and outer beauty inextricably woven. My prayer is that when you tie it all together, the stunning fabric will be a healthier, happier, lovelier you.

Beauty may be in the eye of the beholder. But there's *more* to beauty than what meets the eye!

La Verne

A Healthy Beginning

BENEATH THE SURFACE

If we imagined a multitiered structure of beauty, health would be the tier just beneath the surface. How well we take care of our body determines the luster of our hair, the clearness of our skin, the resilience of our nails. In the pursuit of beauty, health is the foundation, the prerequisite.

Webster's Ninth New Collegiate Dictionary defines health as "the condition of being sound in body, mind, or spirit; *esp.:* freedom from physical disease or pain." The beauty world redefines health as "wellness," suggesting not only the absence of sickness, but impling the presence of lifestyles which make living more enjoyable. This section is devoted to exploring just that.

A stressed, fatigued, undernourished body will block the ultimate path to health and beauty. Poor eating habits result in nutritional deficiencies. The effects eventually show up as disfiguring facial acne, stunted hair growth and nails which are thin and brittle.

To start this section, diet makeover Juanda Green stars with her determination to lose unwanted pounds and win in self-esteem. We've captured her step-by-step story in photos showing a great body becoming even more beautiful.

How to use "Nutrition Against Disease" and pamper your heart to health is an indispensable lifetime guide with information from Black family physicians. Their expert advice for smart eating is just what the doctor ordered.

Well, that's a lot to digest. Here's to your health!

See the complete story of Juanda Green's Diet-Makeover in the color section. Photo: George Selman

LOSING TO WIN

What does it take to feel good about yourself? For some women, it takes less —much less weight.

If you have pounds to shed, here are basic diet tips to help you. A diet makeover's testimony demonstrates that losing pounds to win self-esteem is key to inner—and outer—beauty!

ANOTHER DIET?

Bookstores abound with diet books, and every year there's a new way to battle the bulge. Providing a specific diet is not the goal of this chapter. Eating preferences and health considerations vary from person to person. Your doctor can help you choose the diet that's best for you.

What you will find here is inspiration and applause! You'll learn how to make dieting an enjoyable adventure as new disciplines give lighter shape to a healthier future. Developing sensible eating habits to last a lifetime should be the *primary* purpose of any diet.

TIPS FOR A LIFETIME

Weight control is not a preoccupation with being skinny. Instead, it's a lifestyle change to safeguard against poor health and fatigue.

Francis O'Neil, a registered dietician at the Pritikin Health and Fitness Center in Los Angeles, says, "Developing eating habits you can live with happily means getting back to the basics—fresh foods, whole grains, fruit and vegetables, nonfat dairy products, fish, poultry and a minimum of red meat."

Since everyone's stomach clock differs, O'Neil recommends having small meals throughout the day. "Tune in to your own physiological needs and bypass the cues which say, 'It's time to eat.' Listening to your body is the best safeguard against overeating.''

Here are some additional tips:

- A one-to-two-pound weight loss per week is a safe goal.
- Preplan your food intake to take the wind out of your impulses.
- Eat only what you need and congratulate yourself for leaving the rest.
- Eat slowly.
- Let the fork rest until you've completely swallowed. In the case of a sandwich, replace it on the plate between bites.
- Drink lots of water—eight glasses a day.
- Gradually increase physical activity.
- Instead of taking the elevator, walk up and down stairs to burn extra calories.
- Schedule time for exercise every day. Choose a sport you really like so that exercising is truly enjoyable.
- Get an exercise buddy.

KEEP A JOURNAL

Keep a journal to record what you eat. Write down your feelings during times of frustration instead of taking them out on food. When you are struggling, review your past successes, no matter how small. They may be just the encouraging push you need.

Becoming more attractive may increase fears of rejection—or acceptance! As body image changes, you may find that professional counseling will help you to better adjust.

Remember, you will hit peaks and valleys during the course of your diet. But don't despair. Just because you blow it for one meal, or one day, or one week, doesn't mean you have to give up entirely. Put the fork down and start again.

DIET MAKEOVER

To demonstrate how dramatic weight loss can be, Juanda Green, a single mother who is completing graduate school, agreed to accept the challenge of a new image. What made her right for this task were these two factors: Juanda demonstrated an admirable degree of self-confidence; and she was ready for a major change in her life.

At twenty-eight years old and five feet four inches tall, Juanda was 188 pounds when she began her diet. First, she consulted her doctor, who administered a series of tests to preclude the possibility of any health-related reason for her weight gain. He recommended vitamins and minerals to replace years of nutritional deficiencies due to poor eating habits.

Next, "before" pictures were taken and they did more than record her story in the making. Juanda kept several snapshots handy and used them as incentive whenever she felt like giving up. Ten months later, and minus forty-plus pounds, she is dramatically shapelier and definitely happier.

GETTING STARTED

After years of accepting herself as overweight, Juanda admits that getting started was the most difficult part of all. It's easy to see how most diets are postponed waiting for the empty refrigerator. The resolve to lose those extra pounds becomes buried in leftovers.

"The feeling that you have to eat in order not to waste food is a good excuse to overeat," says Juanda, "but I've learned that eating is not the way to prevent waste. If I eat, it will still be a waste—right on my waistline!"

Juanda had thought that dieting was a short-term task, rather than a lifetime discipline. "At the beginning of my diet, I didn't realize I'd have to have such tenacity to follow through. But I needed time to develop new attitudes about food, new ways to think about eating. Even when I reach my goal of 130 pounds, maintaining my weight will happen at every meal throughout my lifetime."

Arike Logan, M.D., a member of the board of directors at King-Drew Medical Center in Los Angeles and a family physician in private practice, suggests that instead of changing your diet overnight, changing gradually makes the adjustment more palatable. For instance, to cut down on your fat intake, try just two or three ounces of red meat only a few times a week, rather than six or eight ounces of meat. As in every area of life, moderation should always be the rule.

"Once a woman realizes how good she feels, she may decide to center her diet on fresh fish and poultry. Even if she doesn't, though, cutting back on red meat minimizes the overall amount of fat in her diet."

Dr. Logan says that the smartest shopper will purchase fresh fruits and vegetables. Like the woman who shops with coupons and realizes these tiny savings add up to many dollars over weeks of shopping, buying fresh foods can add up to healthy benefits in years to come.

Steaming fresh vegetables for just a few minutes, rather than boiling the nutrients to the bottom of the pot, is one way to enhance the dining experience. "And because so many women work or are busy during the daytime, steaming is one change which may be easiest to incorporate at dinnertime since it's quicker than boiling," says Dr. Logan.

To add icing to her advice, Dr. Logan recommends skipping dessert. "It's not necessary to have dessert after *every* meal. If there is a taste for something sweet, a piece of fruit can satisfy just as well."

VITAMINS AND MINERALS

For the next step, vitamins and minerals were recommended to Juanda to replace years of nutritional deficiencies caused by poor eating habits.

"A primary source of vitamins and minerals is the foods we eat," says Judith S. Stern, Sc.D., professor of nutrition at the University of California at Davis.

"Rather than relying totally upon supplements, most experts recommend getting nutrients directly from foods. But in certain situations such as weight loss, or pregnancy or while taking some medications, additional supplements can be helpful. So that you don't oversupplement first check with your physician."

Dr. Stern explained that the woman on a diet is losing weight because she is probably consuming less than 1,800 calories a day. But by eating fewer calories, she is also reducing her intake of vitamins and minerals.

Even when not dieting, some women may be eating on the run and skipping meals altogether, and a daily supplement may be beneficial. But what is detrimental is an effort to overcompensate by taking megadoses of nutrients—up to ten times the U.S. Department of Agriculture's recommended dietary allowance, or RDA, which refers to the amount of nutrients a healthy person needs. A multivitamin and mineral supplement taken once daily should not exceed the U.S. RDA.

In addition to her daily multivitamin, Juanda supplements her diet with a *vitamin B complex.* Beneficial for the heart, muscles, and nerves, the B vitamins—B_1 (Thiamin), B_2 (Riboflavin), B_3 (Niacin), B_6 and B_{12}—energize the body by assisting foods to release energy. B Complex also helps hair and nails to grow by forming healthy red blood cells which supply oxygen to the tissues.

Juanda's personal physician also added *vitamin C* to her daily supplements. Vitamin C helps the formation of collagen, the glue that holds skin together.

Because C raises the white blood cell content, it also helps wounds heal and militates the body in resisting infection, hence its reputation as a cold-fighter. While vitamin C may not actually prevent a cold, it may lessen the severity of cold symptoms.

While it's prudent to have a daily source, megadosing on C can cause kidney and bladder stones, diarrhea and urinary tract irritation. The RDA for vitamin C is 60 milligrams, with an additional 20 milligrams for pregnant women and nursing mothers.

Ideally, a well-balanced diet should supply a sufficient amount of the minerals—calcium, magnesium, zinc, iron—a body needs. But because iron is lost through menstruation, most women find it difficult to get enough. A daily supplement rounds out Juanda's regimen.

The RDA for iron is 18 milligrams for women aged nineteen to fifty and 10 milligrams over age fifty-one. A daily supplement of 30 to 60 milligrams is normally recommended for pregnant and nursing women. Vegetarians and dieters may also need an iron supplement, but megadoses of iron can cause bacterial and fungal infections.

FOOD SOURCES

Dr. Stern stresses that the best source of vitamins and minerals comes from eating a balanced diet. "With the proper combination of foods, vitamins and minerals work together to complement each other," she says.

Because no pill has it all, reliance upon supplements is not a guarantee that you are getting all the essential nutrients your body needs. A daily variety of foods from the *Basic Four Food Groups,* with an emphasis on fruits, vegetables and whole grains, forms the basis of good nutrition:

- **Dairy**—2 servings a day (includes yogurt, hard cheese, cottage cheese).
- **Lean meat/fish/poultry**—2 servings of protein, with only one third to one half from animal sources (to minimize the amount of fat, calories and cholesterol) and the rest from vegetable sources (dried beans and peas, nuts and seeds).
- **Vegetable/fruit**—4 servings, including one naturally rich in vitamin C (such as guava or orange juice) plus one deep yellow or dark green vegetable.
- **Bread/cereal/grains/pasta**—4 servings of whole grain or enriched, plus one serving of whole grain.

Whole grains, pasta, enriched cereals and breads, brown rice, dark green vegetables, lima beans, green beans, soy beans, peas, mushroom, sweet potatoes, avocados, cheese, eggs, milk, meat, chicken, tuna, turkey, veal, fish, oysters, liver, molasses, oranges, bananas, peanuts, almonds, wheat germ and nutrition yeast are just some examples of foods with B vitamins.

Citrus fruits—kiwi, melon, oranges, grapefruit, guava—cantaloupe, strawberries, turnip greens, broccoli, asparagus, tomatoes, kale, mustard greens, collards and Brussels sprouts are some excellent food sources for vitamin C.

Mother was right when she encouraged you to eat iron-rich liver at least once a week. In addition to being a rich iron source, liver contains a host of other essential nutrients as well. Fish, eggs, molasses, barley, oysters, bananas and most beans such as lima beans and soy beans, almonds, nuts, whole grains, kelp, chard, asparagus and dried fruits such as raisins are also good iron sources.

WATER

Water, essential for proper kidney function, is also important to the dieter. Juanda was reminded to drink lots of water—about six to eight glasses a day—advice which Dr. Stern supports.

"When dieting, since you're eating less, you may forget to drink water. Don't! Water facilitates weight loss and is an important factor in weight maintenance."

AN EXTRA HELPING

For Juanda, holidays and family times are still the most difficult days to diet. "A dinner for two does not pose the temptation for me to cheat. But once I'm around a large group of people who are eating whatever they want, I need an extra helping of self-control. I remind myself that what's a second on my lips is forever on my hips."

Once the excitement of losing the first pounds has passed, patience and endurance—that resolve not to give up—is what overcomes the plateau phase. "It's so frustrating when you are following your diet but the scale remains the same," says Juanda. "Success demands patience."

With an increased energy level, Juanda now enjoys the physical and psychological benefits of regular exercise. An hour at the gym a minimum of three times a week helps carve curves, firm skin and improve muscle tone.

"It's not easy to describe the excitement of being able to wear a sleek, clingy black skirt in a medium size and look good in it! Nothing tastes as good as thin feels!"

And the benefits are internal, too. "I had always secretly been afraid that my weight problem would only gain momentum. But now I have a grip on my weight and I feel better about myself. I've lost inches and gained self-esteem."

Juanda is still pounds away from the weight that's right for her height, but already she looks incredible! Because seeing is believing her step-by-step progress and stunning makeover appear in the color section.

WHAT'S REASONABLE?

What weight is reasonable for your height? The chart below from the U.S. Department of Agriculture suggests a weight range for women to be measured, minus shoes and clothing. Their suggestions go only to 5 feet 10 inches tall, but I've expanded the chart to include women up to 6 feet.

REASONABLE BODY WEIGHTS FOR WOMEN

Height (feet, inches)	Weight (pounds)
4'10"	92–121
4'11"	95–124
5'0"	98–127
5'1"	101–130
5'2"	104–134
5'3"	107–138
5'4"	110–142
5'5"	114–146
5'6"	118–150
5'7"	122–154
5'8"	126–159
5'9"	130–164
5'10"	134–169
5'11"	138–174
6'0"	142–179

Note: For women 18–25 years, subtract one pound for each year under 25.
Source: Adapted from the Metropolitan Desirable Weight Table (up to 5' 10").

Remember, when it comes to your weight, it's not a question of loving you the way you are. It's a matter of encouraging you, because you *are* loved, to bring those excess pounds into a healthy perspective.

The benefits are all yours! You'll feel better, and you'll look better, too. Doesn't this sound like the right ingredients for a fuller, happier life?

EATING DISORDERS

Here's a word of caution. Concern about proper weight is not to be confused with an obsession to be skinny-skinny.

Anorexia Nervosa, the self-starvation syndrome, and *bulimia,* binging and purging, are eating disorders rooted in the intense fear of becoming obese. Even as weight loss progresses, a woman may look emaciated, yet the fear of being fat does not diminish.

Excessive exercise often accompanies such eating disorders. Serious physical problems result, and the untreated condition can lead to severe complications, even death.

It's difficult to treat anorexia nervosa or bulimia without professional counseling. A hospital therapy program which combines nutrition management, weight restoration, stress reduction, support groups and a controlled exercise program can usually be completed on an outpatient basis.

If you have a friend who is suffering, don't avoid the problem. Voice your concern and, above all, encourage her to get help.

NUTRITION AGAINST DISEASE

Juanda's goal to lose those extra pounds may affect *more* than just her weight. While heredity plays a major role in the onset of hypertension, atherosclerosis and diabetes, there is a significant relationship between poor nutritional habits and poor health.

HEREDITY AND DIET

It is true that major illnesses are caused by many factors and are not solely dependent upon what we do or do not eat. Heredity—those health patterns we see in our parents and grandparents—plays the bigger role.

However, a smart diet is one common-sense prevention we can all incorporate into our lifestyle. While researchers are still examining the strong correlation among heredity, nutrition and disease, the evidence is stacked high against an excess of sugar, salt, fat and cholesterol in our diet.

"By drastically reducing your intake of fats, oils, meats and other foods high in cholesterol, you will not only look and feel better, but you will also reduce the possibility of contracting a variety of illnesses including hypertension, diabetes, atherosclerosis and strokes," says nutrition and heart specialist Tazewell Banks, M.D. He is professor of medicine at Howard University College of Medicine and director of the Central Heart Station at District of Columbia General Hospital.

"There is much that we can do to change the effects of heredity. A low-salt, low-fat, and low-cholesterol diet with moderate exercise and not smoking can minimize, prevent or even reverse the effects of heredity depending on how far you are willing to go."

To underscore his point about looking better, Dr. Banks makes this observation: "Body-builders and tri-athletes are on a low-fat, low-cholesterol, high-starch, high-vegetable and moderately high-fruit diet. The result? They are healthier, slimmer, and they perform better."

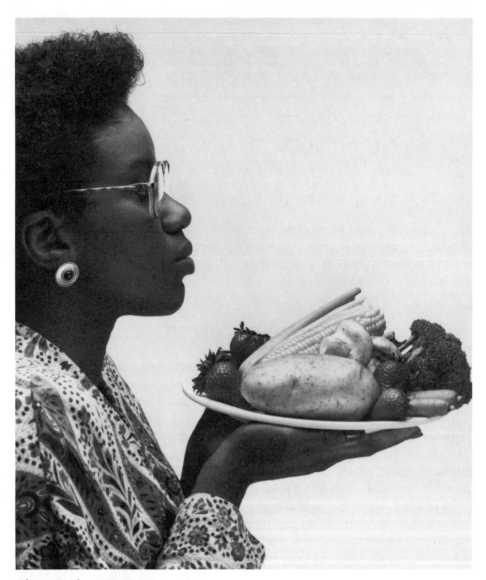

Photo: Barbara Du Metz

On the matter of feeling good, Dr. Banks offers this test. "I challenge any woman to eat a high starch, low fat, low salt and a low cholesterol diet for just three days. This should include rice, other grains, pasta, cereals, green and yellow vegetables and fruit.

"On the fourth day, I ask her to have bacon and eggs with regular milk and butter on her toast for breakfast, a cheeseburger with french fries and a milk shake for lunch. For dinner, have a juicy steak with sour cream on the potatoes. I guarantee that she will feel bad and sluggish by that evening and/or the next morning."

HYPERTENSION

Of the 60 million Americans who suffer from *hypertension,* nearly one third are Black. Because hardening of the arteries is caused by the depositing of fat in the vessels, hypertension is a major risk factor in heart attack, the leading cause of death in this country.

Arike Logan, M.D., explains that hypertension refers to the amount of pressure exerted by the heart to push blood through the system.

"The heart beats, then rests. When measured, the first reading indicates the amount of force with which the heart pushes the blood through the arteries. The second measures the heart at rest. Too much force can strain the heart, causing an enlargement. But other organs may also be affected. The kidneys are very sensitive to pressure, and hypertension can damage them, too."

Controlling obesity is one key to treating hypertension. Even though a woman may be predisposed because of heredity, with weight maintenance her blood pressure may remain normal. Additionally, a report by the American Heart Association shows a direct relationship between alcohol intake and increase in blood pressure.

The high-salt diet has been associated with hypertension. It may be related to the body's inability to handle sodium.

"Some people remain unaffected by high-salt intake while others develop hypertension at a relatively low-salt intake. Heredity may predetermine who can and who cannot tolerate a high-salt diet," says Dr. Logan.

Studies show a strong correlation between the degree of salt intake among various cultures and the occurrence of hypertension in that population. For instance, in the Japanese culture, sodium intake is high, and so is incidence of high blood pressure. On the other hand, hypertension occurs less frequently in European cultures where there is a low-salt intake.

How much salt is enough? The estimated safe daily dietary salt intake is 1,100 mgs. to 3,300 mgs. "But," says Dr. Logan, "for people who are concerned about hypertension, my recommended range is 1,000 to 2,000 mgs. of sodium a day."

To give you an idea of how little salt this is, a single teaspoon of salt is equivalent to 2,000 mgs. of sodium or 5,000 mgs. of salt. In tracking salt intake, though, remember that it's not just the salt that's added at the table.

Consider, too, salt which is already in foods, plus the salt that's sprinkled during cooking.

"When reading labels remember that sodium, another name for *sodium chloride*—salt—is also listed as *Na* or *NaCl,* its chemical symbols," advises Dr. Logan.

Minimizing salt intake is a major safeguard in the fight against hypertension. Fruits and vegetables which are purchased fresh have not been spoiled by the addition of salt as a preservative. When buying frozen foods, select those which are frozen plain—without any sauce.

In general, avoid all prepared foods such as TV dinners and fast foods. Salt is used to enhance flavor in luncheon meats, canned vegetables, canned and packaged soups, peanuts, potato chips and pickles. Oriental dishes made with soy sauce are very high in salt content. One tablespoon of soy sauce has 858 mgs. of salt!

Remove the salt shaker and spice up foods with natural vegetable seasonings instead. Fresh herbs, like garlic, basil and onion, and low-calorie dressings are delicious ways to enhance the natural flavor of foods.

The table below offers a few comparisons of the salt content in fresh, frozen and canned foods.

Fresh	1 small, ripe, raw tomato	3 mgs. salt
Canned	tomato sauce, 1/2 cup	654 mgs. salt
Fresh	1 stalk raw broccoli	15 mgs. salt
Frozen	broccoli in cheese sauce, frozen	350 mgs. salt
Fresh	turnip greens, raw, 1/2 cup, cooked	0 mgs. salt
Canned	turnip greens, canned, 1/2 cup	236 mgs. salt

(Bowe's & Church's Food Values of Portions Commonly Used, by Pennington and Church, J. B. Lippincott Company, ©1980)

ATHEROSCLEROSIS

Also called heart disease, *atherosclerosis* destroys vital blood vessels. Heredity heads the list of major risk factors which influence heart disease.

Close on the heels of heredity is the habit of cigarette smoking. As more and more women choose to smoke, they are closing the gap in the male/female mortality rates in heart attacks, cancer and lung disease due to cigarettes.

"Mortality from heart disease continues to decline in the white population but it has started back up in the last five years for the Black female," Dr. Banks notes.

"This is largely because of increased smoking, obesity, inactivity and diet. No matter how much money a woman spends on cosmetics, clothes or jewelry, if she is not healthy there is no way she can stay vibrant and sensuous."

Besides health concerns, there's the issue of vanity. "Smoking increases facial wrinkling second only to the sun. Moreover, the smell of cigarette smoke on a woman's clothes and hair is a turnoff for a man whose sense of smell has not been dulled from smoking."

Stress and lack of exercise are also risk factors in heart disease. But hypertension and diabetes are bigger determinants in premature heart problems. So, too, is high blood *cholesterol.* Cholesterol, naturally produced by the body, is a wax or glue-like substance which circulates in the bloodstream.

Extra sources of cholesterol are found in foods of animal origin—meat, poultry and dairy products. Egg yolks, shellfish, sardines and organ meats such as brains, liver and kidney are high in cholesterol, too. Luncheon meats such as pastrami, salami and sausage are both salty and fatty.

"Although heart disease probably results from a complexity of problems, there is a high clinical correlation between the risk factor of high cholesterol in the diet and heart disease," says Dr. Logan.

Dr. Banks underscores this point. "Cholesterol is a killer. The fatty substance found in foods such as butter, eggs and meat is the major cause of hardening of the arteries."

He explains why. "Fatty deposits collect on the inner walls of the arteries narrowing the blood vessels. That means that vital organs are deprived of oxygen."

Lowering the level of cholesterol in the diet is smart heart health. The American Heart Association feels that learning to control risk factors now may prevent heart disease in the future.

Some new recommendations by the AHA are:

- Reduce your total fat intake to under 30 percent of calories.
- Avoid eating too many foods containing saturated fat and cholesterol.
- Substitute polyunsaturated fat for saturated fat whenever possible but do not eat too much of any kind of fat.

Saturated fats are mainly animal fats, such as lard. They usually turn white on a plate or harden at room temperature.

Polyunsaturated fats are mainly found in vegetables and cooking oils—safflower, sesame seeds, sunflower seeds, corn, soybeans and cottonseeds—and are liquid at room temperature.

"Avoid any food with a label that says 'animal' or 'animal and vegetable' fats," warns Dr. Logan. "Not only are these foods high in fat content, but they are also high in cholesterol. And remember, while it is a vegetable oil, coconut oil is saturated and appears to be as harmful for the body as lard."

Both doctors encourage us to read labels. A "no-cholesterol" label is not enough. It should also say "polyunsaturated" or "monosaturated." For instance, olive oil is monosaturated and it appears to be helpful.

Dr. Banks cautions us to avoid alcoholic beverages, caffeine drinks and all sodas. He adds, "Drink nonfat skim milk or nonfat buttermilk. Naturally, water is the best drink."

Exercise is as important to heart health as diet. Says Dr. Banks, "Moderate exercise, such as walking briskly with stretching before and after, is good for your heart. Exercise lowers blood pressure, helps with weight reduction, and reduces the progression of atherosclerosis. It also reduces the tendency to and helps in the control of diabetes."

Are these enough reasons to get that body moving? If not, here is a bonus! "For every hour of exercise, you can add that hour plus an additional hour to your life."

DIABETES

Our ethnic group has a 33 percent higher rate of *diabetes* than the general population. And Black women get diabetes at twice the rate of Caucasian women.

Diabetes affects the way the body uses food. In the digestive process, sugars, starches and other foods are changed to a form of sugar called glucose. It is then carried by the blood to the liver as well as to various cells throughout the body. With the help of insulin, a hormone made in the pancreas, the cells use glucose for energy or store it for later use.

In people with diabetes, insulin is either ineffective or lacking altogether. When glucose is unable to enter the cells, it accumulates in the bloodstream and the surplus is eliminated by the kidneys. High levels of sugar in both blood and urine indicate a malfunction in the changeover process and is a sign of diabetes.

There are two types of diabetes. Type I, which occurs in children and young people, is the most serious. The more common Type II is called "adult-onset diabetes." It primarily affects overweight adults.

According to the American Diabetes Association, 80 percent of all adult diabetic patients are overweight at the time of diagnosis. It is believed that many of these cases could be prevented if individuals maintained a desirable body weight and kept physically fit.

If diabetes is part of your family's medical history, careful attention to diet and exercise is important.

"A woman with a history of diabetes in her family should take the extra precaution of having annual checkups and maintaining a normal body weight," advises Carmen H. Grange, M.D., a New York physician specializing in the treatment of diabetes and on the staff at St. Vincent's Hospital.

She suggests that with a family history of diabetes, it's always smart to pass up regular syrup for low-calorie syrup, or heavy, rich desserts for fresh fruit or sherbert. Ice tea or fruit juices, up to a glass per day, are better substitutes for soft drinks that are high in calories.

"And pay attention to labels," says Dr. Grange. "Nutrition labeling is designed to inform you of the ingredients in food. The list begins with the largest amount of an ingredient and ends with the smallest."

If sugar, which is sometimes called *sucrose,* is listed first, then the product has more sugar in it than any other ingredient and should be avoided.

Labels that say "dietetic" or "low-calorie" do not necessarily mean the product is sugar-free. It means that there is less sugar than in the regular product.

Foods which are especially high in saturated fat adversely affect diabetes because excess fat in the system prevents insulin from working properly.

Fried foods are fat-laden. An extra crispy fried chicken dinner, for example, can contain as much as 1,554 mgs. of sodium and 43 grams of fat! It's easy to see why baked or broiled is healthier.

Fast foods are low on nutrients but high in saturated fat, sodium, sugar and calories. Add condiments to fast foods—catsup, mayonnaise, tartar sauce, salad dressings—and the high fat/salt level is hardly worth the convenience.

This is not to suggest that you *never* have that fast, pre-prepared meal, commonly referred to as junk food. But by limiting these meals, we may add years to our life—and *life* to our years!

STRESS

Stress is an underlying factor in major illness. Pressures arise out of the need to survive, out of the anxiety simply to cope.

"Stress can be defined as outside-sourced pressure," explains Rex Johnson, Ph.D., assistant professor of Christian education at Biola University in California.

"Life is full of stress. The person who lives in the country experiences pressure just like the person who lives in the city. Everyday pressures come from situations like working with an unfair boss, hurrying in rush-hour traffic or caring for a disabled child. The source of stress may be different, but the effect of the stress is equal."

Stress, the outside force, pushes, pulls, shoves our last nerve. We respond with anxiety, nervousness, worry, frustration, anger—negative emotions that cause our spirits to sag and our bodies to crumble. While we can't always alleviate the source of stress itself, we can find acceptable ways to help us cope with pressure.

"Stress is the result of inadequately handled reactions to what's going on in your world," says Craig K. Polite, Ph.D., a clinical psychologist specializing in Black middle-class stress in New York City.

"That world can be either internal or external. Similar events may occur in other people's worlds. The difference is that some people handle it while others are handled by it."

Dr. Polite suggests that when we make the time to do what's necessary in order to be well, "we are taking personal responsibility for our lives."

Where can we begin?

Lifestyle changes which emphasize leisure and relaxation can help minimize the effects of stress. Spend more time in a nurturing, caring environment with family and friends. Join professional groups and social organizations, clubs and churches, where common interests and concerns can be shared.

Here are some additional stress-reducing tips:

- In the morning, a fifteen-minute quiet time helps you focus on the day ahead. It may be necessary to get up a little earlier than everyone else just to ensure that your quiet time is *quiet.* If necessary, unplug the phone; declare your designated space "off limits."
- In the afternoon, a nap, no matter how busy you are, does wonders to minimize stress. If you rest fifteen minutes to an hour before picking up the children from school, for instance, they will be the first to notice the difference.
- Carving out daily time for exercise takes the pressure valve off stress. It's a way to positively release pent-up tensions. And, since the focus is on you, you'll not only feel better, you'll look better, too.

The biggest plus is that you'll *be* better! That's what the next section, "Body Works," is all about!

BodyWorks

FIRST IMPRESSIONS

First impressions count, and the appearance of a striking woman takes into account *all* of her—the way she walks, stands, sits, moves. Because she cares about herself, she makes the time to exercise to maintain her physical stamina, personal strength and positive shape.

Although challenge is exciting, her goal is not competition but definition. And because she demands excellence of herself in her home, at school, with her children or on her job, she depends upon excelling by sticking to a tailored regimen that works for her.

Why? A trimmer waist may be the result, but it's not the ultimate goal. Firmer thighs may improve the figure, but the physical benefits are merely by-products. Flexing confidence, tightening self-esteem and developing discipline are the real motivations for sit-ups that make you stand tall *inside*.

This section is called "BodyWorks" because when we work our bodies, our minds become stronger.

Meet Janice Darling, a woman who fought her way back to health with exercise. In these pages she shares her scientific approach for optimum body —and mental—health.

And Miss Olympia, Carla Dunlap, encourages women to develop all they have, including their muscles. As the first Black woman to pump iron professionally, Carla believes that being "buff" is a feminine positive. In these pages, she shares her weight-training philosophy and exercises with you.

With a little commitment, you can rechannel your energies to enhance the shape of your body. That's what this section is all about.

Go ahead. Go for it!

THE PSYCHOLOGY OF EXERCISE

There's more to exercise than just pounding the pavement to fight the flabbies and trim those tummies. Benefits may be visible on the surface, but the real effects reach beyond vanity. The psychology of exercise is not for the sole bonus of looking better. More importantly, exercise makes you *feel* better.

MENTAL HEALTH

On the exercise mat, better mental health wins in the competition for better physical health. Completing just one more repetition, running an additional half mile, bicycling all the way to the top of that hill or swimming an additional lap does more than score victories in the battle of the bulge.

Yes, arms become stronger, waist trimmer, hips firmer and thighs lovelier. But the real psychology behind exercise is what it does *in* you rather than what it does *to* you. The most important muscle is the one that's flexed in the mind.

A commitment to fitness does not mean tipping the scale on the side of obsession. Rather it's a balanced way to release stress, share the comradery of fellow exercise buffs, enjoy music, have fun and, above all, celebrate life.

Emotional benefits soar with exercise. Increased self-esteem is really what it's all about. Women who care about fitness and health are wholesomely attractive, while a woman who is concerned merely about her looks may be overly dependent on cosmetics.

A healthy body and strong bones are what matter most. The bonus is that in addition to feeling wonderful you look great, too!

BEATING THE BLUES

Whether the choice is speed-walking, jogging, bicycling, low-impact aerobics, jumping rope, dance, tennis, racquet ball, swimming or weight training, keeping active is an effective way to beat the blues.

Because of the female cycle, some women experience mood swings. At times poor eating habits or premenstrual syndrome may account for periods of extreme sensitivity.

It may be hardest to work out when feelings of depression and lethargy set up camp in the frontiers of the emotions. But this is when exercise is a most welcome strategy. Without an appropriate outlet, that down-in-the-dumps feeling called *mood depression* may persist, affecting perceptions and hindering performance.

"Depression affects what a woman thinks of herself and how she perceives the world around her," says clinical psychologist Constance Hammen, Ph.D., professor of psychology at UCLA.

"No matter what her reality, a woman who is depressed tends to feel unattractive. In actuality she may be successful, yet she may insist she is inadequate. Her positive qualities are devalued and she magnifies the negative. When it comes to coping with everyday life, depression always tips the scale to the minus side."

Sometimes, there are valid reasons underlying occasional feelings of depression. "Certain losses, such as the ending of a relationship or experiencing the death of a loved one, are life events in which people are expected to suffer from temporary depression," explains Dr. Hammen.

In addition, the day-to-day, month-to-month, year-to-year pressures of mere survival can at times seem too much to absorb. Feelings of hopelessness can become overwhelming and open the door to depression.

THE SYNDROME

A cluster of symptoms points to clinical depression called the *syndrome of depression,* which requires professional help. Loss of appetite alone or occasional insomnia, or an isolated instance of irritability, or short-term social withdrawal does not suggest that a woman is clinically depressed. But a combination of these occurring for an extended period of time might signal trouble.

The syndrome of depression differs from periodic and brief moods of depression in that it lasts longer. Seeking professional help is a sign not of weakness but of strength. It's a positive step up out of the pits.

FITNESS SURVEY

Exercise can be one way to grab mild depression by the ankles and climb out of an emotional rut. That's where the psychology of exercise gets a standing ovation.

A recent fitness survey substantiates that women who are healthy and who feel fit experience fewer moods of depression, loneliness and worthlessness. The survey concludes that the active woman actually feels more attractive and overall is better adjusted.

GO TAKE A WALK

If you've never exercised before, how should you begin? Put on some comfortable walking shoes and go take a walk.

Swing arms, step briskly and hold your head up. Notice how good you feel when you're done.

Don't try to become a marathon walker overnight. Tackle one or two blocks first time out, then increase distance as you feel comfortable. Remember to breathe deliberately as you stride and maintain a brisk pace. When you're ready, maximize calorie burn by carrying one-pound hand-held weights. As you walk, think good thoughts.

Physical fitness supports mental health. Mental health fosters physical health. The benefits are available to anyone who is serious about being sensible.

In the next chapter, see how Janice Darling courageously met the challenge of a shattered life and battled depression through the positive action of exercise.

A DARLING WAY TO EXERCISE

Exercise for your body. And exercise for your mind. That's what Janice Darling teaches.

THE SWEATSHOP

The Sweatshop, "where it's fun to work hard," is an exercise studio in Los Angeles. Its proprietor is Janice Darling, a young Black woman who is a motivational fitness instructor. She believes that exercise attacks depression, increases self-esteem and builds confidence. For Janice the only choice is to flex the muscles in her mind and exercise her courage.

EXERCISE IN COURAGE

She was thirty years old when she lost her daughter, who drowned in a pool accident. Janice plunged into despair. Months later, she looked up to find herself very unhappy, hopelessly out of shape and thirty pounds over-weight.

Encouraged by her husband, she attended acting school and took ballet lessons. But with the excess pounds, she needed to do more than diet to feel comfortable wearing body-baring leotards. Through the effort to lose weight, Janice rediscovered her love of athletics. Long-distance running and high-powered aerobics helped get her body back into shape. She even began teaching class at a popular L.A. studio.

Just when it seemed that she was finally back on track, a near-fatal accident almost shattered her life. While she was standing in a movie line with her husband, a car driven by a drunk driver raced backward out of control, torpedoed from the gas station across the street and crashed onto the side-walk, smashing into the waiting line of people.

Photo of Janice Darling by George Selman. Makeup: Rudy Calvo. Hair: John Atchison

One of the first to be hit, Janice was hurled furiously through a wall of glass which severed a nerve in her left eye. Her eye had to be replaced with a glass eye, but she was grateful just to be alive.

The pelvic injuries were so extensive that doctors admitted it was only her superbly conditioned muscles, strong tendons and firm ligaments that kept everything in place. Though her bones were crushed, her muscles, like faithful guards, literally held her insides together.

Deciding not to focus on the loss of her eye, Janice concentrated on getting the rest of her body back into shape. Her physical therapist suggested she try thirty minutes of exercise and do ten leg lifts a day. But Janice knew that if she was ever to walk again she had to do more. When the therapist left the hospital room, she continued, past the pain, to do additional leg lifts.

By her third week in the hospital, Janice graduated to one thousand leg lifts a day with two-and-a-half-pound weights strapped to her ankles. With determination, and without an operation, Janice was on her feet in a month. She walked out of the hospital, aided only by crutches.

Three months after the accident, she was back teaching exercise class. And her students responded to her powerful encouragement. They knew that being in shape had prepared Janice for this challenge. They saw her push past her own limitations and they could push past theirs, too.

Within weeks her classes were filled to capacity, and the demand for Janice became so great that she had to open her own exercise studio two years later.

CONFIDENCE

"It takes more than will to succeed. It takes confidence," says Janice.

How do you build confidence? "You do something every day to strengthen a part of you. When you need the strength next Monday, it'll be there, like a well-trained muscle. Once it's exercised, all you have to do is flex."

Success, she explains, works the same. You build it daily and when you need to flex it in a difficult situation, it's there.

"I see success as a series of small rituals that culminate in achievement. The little bit I do today gets me to tomorrow. With the completion of each task, I feel more confident as well."

With this motivation, exercise is well worth the effort. "It's not about an emphasis on a small waist or tiny hips. It's much, much more. Exercise sculpts confidence."

Janice Darling's exercises are shared below. Try to work out for thirty minutes at least three or four times a week. Vigorous exercise like aerobics raises levels of *endorphin* in the body and is a natural way to elevate your mood and beat depression.

You are in competition with no one but yourself so set your own pace. But comfortable limits that don't challenge are not the goal. Demand the best of yourself, because the best is what you deserve.

TRIMMING AND TONING

These exercises are targeted to trim and firm hips, thighs and derriere. For the woman who thinks she'll never again have a toned tummy, the abdominal exercises here are guaranteed to make you a believer. Waistline benefits, too.

As you flex and lift, remember to repeat encouraging words to yourself. You *are* getting stronger. You *are* increasing in confidence.

Set a goal for yourself and don't give up until you've reached your objective. And if nothing else, do just one more than yesterday!

DRESSING FOR SUCCESS

If you're serious about exercising for success, then dress for success. "Most people take better care of their cars than their bodies, even though the body is the most basic machine," says Janice.

"If you invest in treatments to make your car look good, why not invest in the right attire so you'll be comfortable *and* look good? It's worth it, and so are you!"

Wearing leotards and tights says you're serious about your workout, even if it's in the comfort of your own home. Because you like the way you look, colorful coordinates can help with motivation, too. It's all part of building that positive self-image. Remember that when you're exercising in cold weather, leg warmers keep muscles—and legs—toasty.

CHALLENGE YOURSELF

As you work each muscle group, think about those muscles. Visualize them getting stronger, firmer. If you are able to work so that you can see yourself in a mirror, check your form; notice the results.

If feelings of laziness creep up, count louder and strengthen your resolve not to give up until you've completed the repetitions.

Do the entire series a minimum of four times a week. Before you begin each session, slowly warm up for at least 10 minutes by doing jumping jacks, running in place or bicycling. Don't work out on an empty stomach; eat a nutritious meal two or three hours before exercising, and drink lots of water.

If you are just beginning a regular program of exercise, check with your doctor before beginning *any* regimen.

THE DARLING ROUTINE

Karen Woods, Esq., is an attorney specializing in federal criminal defense. As a professional woman, Karen believes that women are often judged by their appearance.

"A woman who takes care of her body has a dynamic presence," she says. "It's not enough just to concentrate on the intellectual or emotional needs. Balance demands that you also pay attention to the physical needs as well. With a busy schedule, there is never enough time for exercise so I have to make time. It's one of my priorities."

For Karen, who attends Janice Darling's Sweatshop, exercises that challenge are a welcome stress reliever. She demonstrates the Darling routine below.

Photos are by George Selman.

OBLIQUES—WAISTLINE

When you are exercising the obliques, always pull your abdominal muscles in tightly and hold as you stretch and bend. Build up to 30 of each exercise but only do as many as are comfortable for you. Counting out loud is a good way to remind yourself not hold your breath while exercising.

SIDE BENDS:
Stand with feet 10 inches apart. Bend arms, clasping hands behind head. Now, bend to the right; return upright. Repeat for left side.

SIDE TWISTS:
Standing with feet apart, knees slightly bent, clasp hands behind head and
slowly twist to the right; return to starting position. Repeat, twisting to the
left.

GLUTEUS MEDIUS—SIDE OF THIGHS

*Check body alignment so that back, hips and buttocks are in a line. When
lifting, think "control." Work up to 50 lifts, then build to 100 at a pace that's
comfortable for you. Remember, counting out loud helps you inhale and exhale.*

BENT-LEG LIFTS:
Lie on a padded surface on your side with right leg, hips and waist touching
floor. Rest on right elbow. Bend knees. With flexed ankle, lift left leg about
10 inches; hold for a second and bring it back to starting position; repeat.
Make sure tummy muscles are pulled in firmly as you do this exercise. Turn
on left side; rest on left elbow; with flexed ankle, lift right leg 10 inches;
hold; repeat.

QUADRICEPS—FRONT OF THIGHS

Holding your head up rather than looking down toward the floor gives you the right form for this exercise. The motion should be smooth, not jerky. Begin at your own pace and work up to 30.

THIGH BOUNCE:
Stand with feet apart, knees deeply bent. Place hands on toes or grasp ankles or lower leg. With head up, slowly bounce buttocks down toward floor; hold for a second, release; repeat. Come out of bend by straightening legs completely before raising head up.

HAMSTRING—BACK OF THIGHS

For this exercise, you can either lean down on your elbows or rest on the palm of your hands, whichever is more comfortable. Work up to 50 kicks, then 100, again, counting out loud.

DONKEY KICKS:
In table position with hands and knees resting on floor, lift right leg up toward ceiling so that leg is parallel with body. Bend the leg at the knee, flex at the ankle and hold this position. Now, kick heel toward ceiling, raising entire leg. Keep head up. Repeat for left leg.

ABDOMINALS—STOMACH

This exercise firms the lower abdominals. As you exercise, hold muscles tightly. As you twist from right leg to left, inhale, then exhale. Rest as needed and work up to 30 bicycles, counting every time your right elbow hits the left knee. Flexing at the ankle gives a good stretch for lower stomach muscles.

BICYCLES:
Lie on back with hands clasped behind head. Twisting body and flexing at the ankle, bend your left leg, bringing left knee across chest to right elbow. Lift shoulder and upper back as you try to touch elbow to knee. Release. Twist to the right side, bending right knee to touch left elbow. As you alternate elbows to opposite knees, move slowly and with even motions. Once you touch easily, try reaching elbow past the outside of the knee.

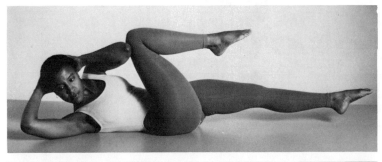

This exercise also works lower abdominals. Work up to 30 lifts with right leg elevated first, then do 30 lifts with left leg elevated.

JACKKNIFE SIT-UPS:
Lie on back with both feet raised toward ceiling, knees locked, ankles flexed. Or, if this is too difficult, bend right leg so that right foot is resting on the

floor supporting lower back. Raise left leg into air with ankle flexed. Enjoy the stretch! Now, with straight arms, reach past legs as if you were trying to touch the wall in front of you. As you reach, lift shoulders and upper back. Exhale with every lift.

Sit-ups carve upper abdominals. Work up to 30 sit-ups, first doing 10 in a row then resting briefly. Once again, keep abdominals pulled in tightly.

BASIC SIT-UPS:
Lie on back with knees bent, feet flat on the floor. Fold arms across chest. Keep feet and arms stationary. Slowly curl, lifting head and shoulders up from the floor only about 5 inches.

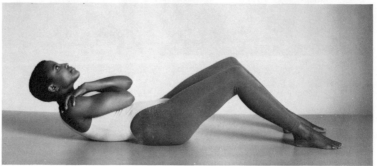

GLUTEUS MAXIMUS—BUTTOCKS

When you lift legs, point toes and keep legs straight. Work up to 20 lifts.

LEG LIFTS:
Lie on your stomach, resting chin on the back of your hands. Hold abdominals tight, squeeze buttocks and lift legs together keeping them in the air for a few seconds. Release; repeat.

Begin with 10 without stopping. Then work up to 20. You may want to try the variation of laying head on the floor and tucking hands under pelvic bones to minimize difficulty.

POINT AND FLEX:
In the same position as for leg lifts, raise legs together as above. Hold; point and flex, point and flex; continue, making sure each movement is well defined.

COOL DOWN

Congratulations! You did it! Now celebrate as you stretch to cool down. Repeat stretch exercises until you feel totally relaxed. As you wind down, tell yourself something beautiful.

SIDE STRETCH:
Sit with legs in a wide V. Lift right arm over head and slowly stretch to the left in a graceful motion. Inhale; exhale. Repeat for other side.

FRONT STRETCH:
Sit with legs pointed straight in front of you. With arms straight, reach up, lifting from hips so that you feel the stretch all the way to the top of your

spine. Now, stretch forward but don't strain; inhale, exhale, as you hold for a few seconds.

Now, give yourself a hug, because you know what? You're better today than you were yesterday!

LEG WEIGHTS

Once you've mastered the legwork, you may want to add weights to your ankles to increase the level of adversity. When it comes to adding those extra weights, Janice cautions you to watch how your body responds.

To guard against straining muscles, begin with half-pound weights which strap firmly around each ankle, and add more—one half pound per leg —only when you can do lifts comfortably and without pausing.

Because weights also help tone tummy muscles, you'll want to be certain your stomach and lower back are in good condition as well. If you're a novice at these exercises, do yourself a favor and wait before adding weights.

Ready for another challenge? It's waiting for you in the next chapter . . .

POETRY IN MOTION

To watch Carla Dunlap perform in body-building competitions is to see poetry in motion. Her excellence is a combination of fluid movements from her love of dance, quiet grace from her mastery of aquatics and proportioned muscles carved from professional weight training. Carla has *something* to flex.

Photo of Carla Dunlap by George Selman. Makeup: Rudy Calvo. Hair: John Atchison

CARLA DUNLAP

Born and raised in Newark, New Jersey, the athletic Carla Dunlap began competition in gymnastics and speed swimming at the age of ten. To merge her love of gymnastics with aquatics, Carla included the graceful art of synchronized swimming into her repertoire.

Earning a degree in advertising from the Newark School of Fine and Industrial Arts was not enough to pull Carla into the currents of the business world. Following graduation, she joined a national swimming team and continued competitive swimming.

Carla's breathtaking mastery won her a gold medal in the Junior National Team Championship and a bronze at the National Sports Festival. By age twenty-five, she was ready to hang up her swimsuit and retire from the pool.

At the urging of a photojournalist, Carla entered her first body-building contest, although she had never previously trained in the sport. Her exquisitely proportioned and muscular frame, taut from years of gymnastics, aerobics and swimming, placed her fifth in a field of forty-five contestants.

Among the host of titles she has since captured are the coveted World Professional Championships, the Miss Olympia crown and the Caesars World Cup Invitational.

A FEMININE POSITIVE

Carla Dunlap is evidence that strength is a feminine positive. "The goal of body-building is to achieve symmetry which is aesthetically beautiful. It's very exciting to develop your body to its maximum potential."

She explains that individual body size and personal preference are determinants in enhancing strength and improving shape. Since everyone already has muscles, sculpting and toning them does not have to mean adding bulk.

Hormones are strategic to the body's ability to become muscular. High levels of androgen, the male hormone, assist men in developing that masculine physique. With females, the level of androgen is only 1 to 5 percent that of the level in men, so the possibility of becoming too muscular is very slim.

"But body-building isn't just for building muscles. If you have the power to change something as close to you as your body, then you can change other areas of your life as well. You realize it *is* possible to achieve success. Self-esteem, self-confidence and self-assurance are what develop the biggest muscles."

Rather than working from the inside out, Carla says body-building works the other way around. "It works from the outside in. First you change your body. Then you begin to change inside."

PUMPING IRON

Aerobic exercise, which burns fat and increases heart and lung capacity, is important to cardiovascular fitness. Carla stresses that pumping iron is in addition to, not in place of, aerobic workouts.

"Any exercise that changes and improves the condition of your physique is body-building. Visualize it in that sense and you'll see all fitness activities in a different light."

But since dance, running and bicycling put upper body work in second place, Carla suggests weightlifting to reduce underarm flabbiness.

For beginners, hand-held weights or dumbbells can be very effective in carving curves. Carla cautions that for upper-body sculpting, more weight is not necessarily better. Heavier weight builds the kind of strength suitable for professional body builders, but for shaping and toning, light to moderate is right.

You should be able to comfortably complete 8 to 10 repetitions, or *reps.* If you can pump up to 15, then the weight is too light for you.

A *set* refers to the number of times you complete 8 to 10 reps. Three sets provide enough resistance without straining muscles. Once you've achieved your desired definition, maintain your shape by doing reps with the same amount of weight.

Carla stresses the importance of warming up muscles before lifting any weights. Avoid rapid movements, which may jerk or strain muscles, and remember to work slowly and thoughtfully. If you have had a muscle strain or any other joint or ligament injury, do not use weights unless in cooperation with a physical rehabilitation therapist.

Women with a family or personal history of heart problems or hypertension should not use weights. And even if these illnesses are not part of your medical history, it is imperative to have a checkup and lift weights *only* with your doctor's permission.

Not to be neglected is proper nutritional intake. "Muscles need nourishment, so the importance of eating correctly cannot be stressed enough," she advises.

BICEPS, TRICEPS AND STOMACH

Believing that body-building is "the best thing to happen to the female body since the aerobics craze," Carla shares three of her favorite body-sculpting exercises.

The Shoulder Press concentrates on firming shoulder, upper back and triceps muscles. The Biceps Curl with Triceps Kickback is actually two movements in one and should be completed in a continuous, slow motion.

For carving curves in the stomach, Carla's Abdominal Roll is most effective when feet are free and not hooked or anchored. This position ensures that you are using stomach muscles and not relying upon stronger thigh muscles.

No matter how experienced you are, the exercises requiring weights should be supervised by a gym or health club professional. Go through the motions without weights first, then add weights as you are being spotted or checked.

SHOULDER PRESS:
First try this exercise sitting down for extra back support. Using a barbell or dumbbells, press both arms directly upward over the head. Keep back erect and straight. Do not allow back to arch. Then try standing up, and stick with whichever is most comfortable for you. *Note:* With barbells, use weight-training gloves to protect hands from developing calluses.

BICEPS CURL WITH TRICEPS KICKBACK:

This combination exercise for the arms combines two movements: First, stand with knees slightly flexed, feet locked and apart and waist bent so that the upper part of the body is parallel to the floor. Holding dumbbells so that arms are pointing downward, bend from the elbow and slowly lift the weight to the shoulder. This exercise should be done with control, and the upper part of the arm should remain still. Next, in one motion, lower the dumbbell back to the starting position and, keeping arms straight, gently lift arm backward. Repeat for other arm.

ABDOMINAL ROLL:

Do not use weights for this exercise. Sit down with knees bent, feet flat on the floor, legs opened to a 45-degree angle, so that your body forms a triangle. Fold arms across chest, contract your pelvic area as if you were trying to push your stomach into your back. Tuck chin down onto your chest and roll back, vertebra by vertebra. Try to press only the small of the back to the floor and lower. Do this very slowly and hold to a count of 10. Release slowly.

EXTRA TIPS

Carla offers these extra tips. Alternate between indoor and outdoor activities to maintain the excitement—and challenge—of staying in shape.

"Never quit altogether, even if you become bored," she cautions. "It's more difficult to get back into shape and you'll lose the physical conditioning you've worked so hard to develop."

And don't be afraid to try something new, or even to compete! "Local competitions are excellent grounds for personal enrichment. It's not winning that's important. Just taking part can be so rewarding. You'll broaden your horizons and meet new, interesting people you never would have met in the normal course of your everyday life."

If weight training is not for you, there are so many other options for building strength, stamina and self-esteem.

"No matter what your decision, do *something.* Because when you exercise, you feel good about yourself."

The weight of Carla's advice cannot be ignored. The sheer enjoyment of staying in shape, plus strengthening yourself *inside,* is what total fitness is all about.

Hair Care

FREEDOM! VERSATILITY! EXCITEMENT!

For years, we as Black women have demanded more for our hair. Freedom, versatility and excitement are musts.

The good news is, we've got it! Improved products increase our flexibility in care and styling options. And we have learned to work with, not against, the unique texture that makes our hair so distinctive.

Our hair is fragile, and we are still learning what it means to handle with care. In this section, "The Language of Beauty" suggests lovely ways to shape our attitudes and build positive images about our hair. Because beauty is from the inside out, how our hair looks to us outside, begins with how we feel about our hair inside.

In "Sleeping Pretty," easy setting tips replace the outdated—and damaging—nighttime roller set. Also included is a discussion of the common ways we can inadvertently break our hair.

Next, treatments that fit your lifestyle offer styling versatility. What's best for you?

Today, relaxers have built-in conditioners and are better than ever. But what's the *real* truth about no-lye? The answer is here. You'll also learn the best way to put needed moisture back into relaxed hair.

And here's the excitement! Today's method of press and curl leaves hair bouncy and oil-free. The chapter "Warm Pressing" also has a salon-recommended conditioning treatment which is ideal for pressed hair.

Natural hair is still "Turning Heads" and works for the lifestyle of many. Fashion and beauty model Peggy Dillard shares her special tips along with her personal "recipe" for natural hair.

With such freedom of choice, the only beauty standards to follow are the ones we set!

THE LANGUAGE OF BEAUTY

Our attitudes about our hair are shaped from the images around us. Magazines, billboards and television all convey messages about what is beautiful and what is not.

We also form impressions from childhood. When our grandmothers and mothers combed and styled our hair, was it a pleasant experience?

While there is little that we can do to change the world around us overnight, there is much that we can do to reinforce our own positive attitudes. When we talk about our hair, we should use words that express the beauty that is ours and ours alone. It's the language of beauty.

GREAT HAIR

Hair that is in healthy condition, that is properly cut, styled and cared for is great hair. Hair that is very curly is especially great, because tight curls are a genetic adaptation to our ancestors' sunny environment. The alternating curly-wave pattern forms a thick, protective barrier which is the most effective way to protect the head against the sun's penetrating, damaging rays.

Not all of our hair has the same curly-wave pattern. Sometimes the curl is close to the scalp and the ends are wavy. Or the curls can be away from the scalp, with waves closest to the scalp. Hair that is wavy or that has large curls or that is very curly or naturally straight represents the distinctive variety of a unique people. It's all *great* hair!

WASH OR SHAMPOO?

The words we use are so important in shaping our feelings. What we say can actually affect the way we handle our hair. Do we wash our hair? Or do we *shampoo?*

Because of the curly-wave pattern, our hair tends to be very, very fragile. The tight curls actually loop into each other. Hair tangles easily and
breaks. Even when the curl is released temporarily or permanently, hair
should be delicately handled.

Washing implies a scrubbing and tugging that is too harsh for our hair.
But when we think "shampoo," we may inspire a more gentle cleansing.
Besides, shampoo sounds prettier.

Frequent shampooing, at least once every four or five days, cleanses hair
of *sebum,* which is the scalp's natural oil. A buildup of sebum combines with
exfoliated or dead skin cells and causes flaking. Add to that hairspray and
hairdressing, and it's easy to see why shampooing often is important. Scalp
feels cleaner, and hair is shinier and more manageable.

Your shampoo should be pH-balanced. If you wear your hair relaxed,
the shampoo should be a conditioning shampoo especially formulated for
relaxed hair. Alternate with a once-a-month deep-cleansing shampoo.

Too much conditioning causes a waxy buildup on hair and scalp. This
coating weighs down hair and makes it appear dull and lifeless. If hair feels
mushy when it's wet, your shampoo may be leaving a coating that's too
heavy. If hair feels brittle and coarse, the shampoo may be too harsh.

Ask your stylist to recommend products for you. You might like to
continue your salon regimen at home and use products that are complemen-
tary to your salon treatments. Always follow every shampoo with a cool
rinse. This helps hair to reflect light easier so it looks shinier, healthier.

PATTING VS. RUBBING

Wet hair is fragile and stretches very easily. Too much tension and pulling can cause hair strands to snap!

When you emerge dripping from shower or sink, never but *never* take a
towel and rub hair vigorously! Rubbing can actually tear your hair. Instead,
pat hair dry or wrap your head in a towel for a few seconds so that the excess
water can be absorbed by the towel.

When you have your hair shampooed at a salon, it's never rude to
remind the person shampooing your hair to be gentle with the towel. Not
only will you prevent breakage, you will also prevent unnecessary tangling.
Your suggestion may be well appreciated, and remember, it's your beauty
dollar.

To comb wet hair, begin at the longest end, away from the scalp, and
always use a wide-tooth comb. If you are wearing a natural, use a metal, not a
wood, pick. A cream rinse will make combing easier.

Never force a comb through your hair. And never, but never, brush wet
hair. When you do brush, keep it to a minimum and select a brush that has

rounded tips. Brushes with plastic bristles can cause breakage and split ends.

As we think fragile, our actions will be gentle. The next chapters offer treatment options—relaxed, pressed or natural—for the world's greatest hair!

SLEEPING PRETTY

Setting hair and sleeping pretty is a combination that can be challenging at best. Here are a few simple tips that liberate us forever from the old-fashioned ritual of sleeping in rollers.

NIGHTTIME DAMAGE

Remember that because our hair is so curly in its natural state, it is more fragile than any other hair. The curls tend to snap easily when combed or brushed. Even when relaxed temporarily or permanently, hair should still be handled with care.

More damage to fragile hair occurs at nighttime than at any other time. Sleeping in those simple little helpers called rollers is more often than not the cause of breaking hair and splitting ends.

Sponge rollers cause the worst nightmare. Because fragile hair tends to be porous, it sticks to a sponge roller like glue. When the roller is removed, tiny pieces of hair adhere to the sponge. If breakage occurs at the end of the hair, the result is frayed, split ends. If breakage is in the middle of the hair strand, the rest of the strand comes out in the brush.

Because the same trauma to the hair is repeated as often as hair is set with sponge rollers, hair never has an opportunity to recover. Every time a roller-set head turns on the pillow, hair breaks little by little.

In addition, sleeping in rollers pulls out hair from around the edges of the hairline. If hair is sparse at the sides but healthy everywhere else you know the damage results from rollers. Once the practice stops, hair will grow back over a period of time.

There is *never* a right time to wear sponge rollers, and sleeping in them is *always* the wrong thing to do for healthy, lovely hair.

Although sleeping in plastic or mesh rollers is not quite as damaging, they, too, break fragile hair. Soft fabric-covered rollers are among the newer

Photo of Sheila Frazier by George Selman

solutions now on the market and may increase the choices for setting delicate hair at night.

Happily, however, there is a prettier, and more romantic, alternative.

PRETTY PIN CURLS

They're easy to do and comfortable to sleep in, and your hair will love them night after night.

Bruce Clark, my hairstylist when I lived in New York, told me about pin-curling my hair almost ten years ago, and I haven't slept in rollers since. So throw away the sponge rollers; pack away the mesh and plastic ones. Pin curls are the prettiest—and best—nighttime set.

There are two types of pin curls. One crisscrosses bobby pins over the rolled curl so that it is completely flat. This gives a texturized look to hair, but this is *not* the pin-curl set that replaces the nighttime roller set.

What does replace the roller set is rolling hair into a barrel curl just as if it were being wrapped over an imaginary roller. Use bobby pins because they are more comfortable than clips. Secure only the part of the curl that lies on the scalp. Do not pin the curl flat or you'll flatten your curl.

Two bobby pins crisscrossed in the inside bottom part of the curl will hold larger curls securely. For tighter curls, use smaller sections of hair.

Set hair in the direction you want it to go in when you comb it out in the morning. Now, sleep prettily!

A LITTLE NIGHT SATIN

Just as turning up a wool coat collar on a wintry day catches and snaps hair at the back of the head, cotton pillowcases add unnecessary friction which is too abrasive for our hair.

Fragments of hair on the pillowcase tell you there's been damage during the night. And although you may not see the full results today, tomorrow's dull-looking condition might be convincing evidence that cotton, no matter how soft, just isn't soft enough.

A little satin at night is like music to your hair. Satin pillowcases are smooth, luxurious treats that won't catch and pull, break or tear your curls. In addition to being one of the best choices a Black woman can make for her hair, sleeping on satin feels absolutely wonderful!

It's easy to substitute a satiny-textured pillowcase for the real thing. In fact, these synthetic pillow covers have that smooth, shiny finish and are just as excellent for your hair. They're quite inexpensive, too, and let you sleep just as beautifully.

QUICK MORNING SET

If you prefer a roller set, this quick morning set will put the bounce back into your curls, accomplishing in ten minutes what normally takes eight hours.

Now is when your plastic or metallic rollers come in handy. Completely submerge them in very hot water for just five minutes.

Remove rollers one at a time and shake excess water or quickly blot dry before setting hair, making sure rollers are still warm. When rolling is complete, protect set with a shower cap before stepping into tub or shower. The additional steam will help hair set quickly. But since steam will also cause hair to revert, do not remove the shower cap until you are out of the bathroom.

Once your bath or shower is complete, wait a few minutes after drying

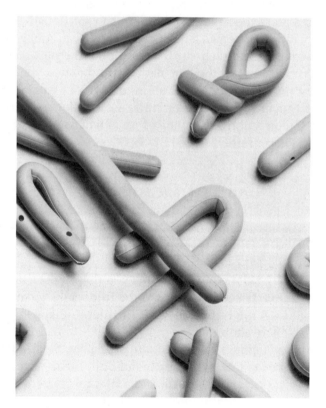

Benders by Clairol. Photo: George Selman

off before removing the rollers so that your body—and your set—has cooled down sufficiently.

STYLING HELPS

If electric rollers are your favorite A.M. standby, always use end papers to protect the ends of your hair. Newer electric rollers look more like big perm rods and are perfect for giving your hair tight curls. And they're great for hair that's cut very short. Since they put the curl in quickly, you only have to leave them in for a few minutes, but you should still use end papers.

Too much heat exposure will dry and split hair over a period of time. Using hot appliances—blow dryers, curling wands—too often will burn the life right out of your hair.

Other styling helps range from nonflaking styling gels to styling mousses with a touch of shimmering color. However, some mousses contain alcohol and are very, very drying for our hair. Check labels for alcohol content.

NIXING ANOTHER RITUAL

Another nighttime ritual to be happily nixed is oiling the scalp. This practice, which dates back to the early 1900s, was originally meant to prolong the effect of a press 'n' curl between shampoos.

Since heavy pomade helps hair resist the reverting effect of scalp perspiration, in addition to guarding against frizzing caused by humidity, it was applied nightly to coat both hair and scalp. Because oiling the scalp was so necessary in order to maintain the press 'n' curl, it was also mistakenly believed to promote hair growth.

However, according to dermatologists, oiling the scalp is one of the most harmful practices for both hair *and* scalp. Chemicals and perfumes in these products combine with the scalp's natural sebum to clog and choke the hair follicle, dramatically stunting hair growth.

In addition to hair that won't grow, scalp irritation, flaking and dandruff result. Hair grows twice as fast on a scalp that's never oiled!

COMPOUNDING DANDRUFF

If oiling the scalp is used to combat dandruff, the result is quite the opposite. The problem is actually compounded because the added oil dries and adheres to natural oils, creating even bigger flakes on the scalp.

Pomade acne, pimples along the sides of the face and forehead, is what dermatologists term the easily treatable condition which is directly related to applying oils to the scalp. Once the practice stops, skin will clear.

Seborrheic dermatitis, or dandruff, itching and flaking is the result of an excessively oily scalp. Adding oil only makes it worse. Instead, shampoo every four days with a shampoo containing sulfur, salicylic acid, protein and conditioners. See a dermatologist if you suspect pomade acne or seborrheic dermatitis.

If all else fails, a sparing touch of a lightweight moisturizing cream applied *only* on the hair, not on the scalp, can temporarily put the shine back into hair that is dull or lackluster. Avoid heavy oils. They make hair look "untouchable."

For hair that is truly dry, however, there is no better solution than a penetrating conditioning treatment. Here's why:

Moisture escapes from our hair wherever hair turns to twist or curl. So hair not only looks dry, it *is* dry. Conditioners, reconstructors and moisturizers are temporary ways to put the moisture back into hair.

The following chapters on relaxed, pressed and natural hair suggest which treatments are best for you.

RELAXERS THEN AND NOW

What's new about relaxers? They are better than ever! Improvements resulting from research and hair technology give us products that condition while relaxing so that hair looks beautiful naturally. Here's a little history explaining relaxers then, and now.

A SOAPY BEGINNING

According to popular legend, relaxers have a soapy beginning which bubbles back to the deep South.

An important ingredient in all soap is sodium hydroxide, or lye. When stirred into the huge iron kettles which sat in the backyard, measurements of sodium hydroxide varied from pot to pot.

It was noticed that over a period of time, the stronger batch of soaps had an unusual effect on tight, curly hair. Not only did it clean, it also straightened—permanently. In the bathtub, the concept for relaxing hair was born.

Although relaxers today contain only 2 to 3 percent sodium hydroxide, early formulations were little more than crude mixtures. Relaxers were actually creamy soaps with a high content of sodium hydroxide.

In the 1930s and '40s, the first commercial relaxers, popularized by Black men, were used in barbershops. And it was not long before relaxing made its Hollywood debut. Stars such as George Raft sported the straight, slicked-down style. "Japping" soon became one of the colloquialisms which meant Black men's hair could now be made as straight as Oriental hair.

Women were slow to follow. Relaxers' popularity had not yet carried over into beauty salons, where Madame C. J. Walker's technique of pressing and curling the hair was still preferred. Since the relaxer had to be left on longer for women, because their hair is thicker than men's, press 'n' curl afforded more control with less chance of damage.

Photo: Eric Bowman. Courtesy Vogue, *December 1986. Copyright* © *Condé Nast Publications, Inc.*

MAKING WAVES

Meanwhile, the men were making waves. During the 1950s, "finger-waving" became popular with Black barbers in New York City, who set the waves with their fingers before drying hair under hooded dryers. Sugar Ray Robinson, the legendary prizefighter, was among the first to popularize this style.

With men now wearing their hair two and a half to three inches long and enjoying the styling freedom afforded by permanently relaxed hair, women finally began to take notice.

Rather than reinvent the wheel in the beauty salon, they began to patronize the barbershops. Setting hair with rollers took the place of finger-waving, ushering in a new era in styling options for women.

By the mid-1950s, Johnson Products, Summit Laboratories and Posner had begun to supply sodium hydroxide relaxers to the beauty salon. While this was a bonus for the client, the Black hairdresser had to make a quantum leap from hot combs to chemical relaxers almost overnight.

The transition was not easy. Applying a protective petrolatum base was necessary prior to applying the relaxer, so the procedure was time-consuming and a bit messy. It took a system of trial and error—overrelaxing and underrelaxing—to perfect the technique of permanently relaxed hair.

By 1965, new improved formulations which did not require a petrolatum base before application captured the market, liberating both stylist and client. Now that stylists understood the product better, they became more adept at correctly applying relaxers. And women felt so secure with the product that the home-use relaxer business became big business.

Perhaps the most exciting advances in the market today are creamy emulsion state-of-the-art relaxers containing built-in moisturizers. With this type of relaxer, the conditioning properties are locked inside the hair shaft *during* the relaxing process. The result: hair is bouncy, has natural shine and healthy luster.

THE TRUTH ABOUT NO-LYE

Because of damage due to improper application stemming from the early days, relaxers have been given a bad rap.

To ease consumer worries, some products are labeled *"no lye"* in an attempt to convince women that there is nothing damaging or harmful in the product. Unfortunately, this is not quite the truth.

Some no-lye relaxers contain two ingredients, *calcium carbonate* and *guanidine hydroxide.* When mixed together, these chemicals become *calcium hydroxide.* Calcium hydroxide is another form of lye, and *that's* the truth.

Few women realize that their "no-lye" relaxer does indeed have a lye content. So they tend to leave the product on longer. Hair can become overrelaxed and damaged as a result.

BEFORE YOU RELAX

For economic or time-saving reasons, many women choose to relax their hair at home. Before you relax, get your hairstylist's O.K. to ensure that your hair and scalp are in healthy condition.

Then, if you are adept at handling your own hair, it is possible to get good results. But remember, a relaxer is a chemical, and one is hard pressed to replace the professional stylist who has had years of experience using the product.

Instructions on home relaxer kits illustrate how to part hair in four major sections. However, it is imperative to *change* the parts from time to time so that you are not always beginning in the same place.

Over a period of months, or years, that thinning which occurs in the middle of the scalp may be due to the relaxer's being left on longest on the same section every time you relax.

Rotate. Begin the relaxer in a different area than you did last time, leaving for last the area you usually relax first.

Here are some additional tips:

Never . . .
- relax your hair at home if you are relaxing it for the first time. Have it done professionally.
- relax if you are growing out another chemical, such as a curly perm.
- relax if hair is damaged with dry or split ends. Your hair should be in excellent condition if you choose to relax at home.
- relax if scalp is irritated, scratched or bruised. First, see a dermatologist.
- relax immediately after removing braids or cornrows. Your hair has been "pulled" and the tension may have made your scalp extremely sensitive. Wait at least six weeks, then consult the experts.
- relax at home if you have *permanent* haircolor. The additional chemical will again break or reform hair bonds, which have already been broken by the coloring process. Breaking bonds again means disintegration, and *that* means more hair will probably be in your brush than on your head.
- retouch too often. If there is not at least half an inch of new growth, you will risk the danger of overlapping, weakening hair

which has already been relaxed. The result will be frizzy, dry, brittle, breaking hair. Mark your calendar and retouch every six weeks.

Always . . .

- ask your stylist's opinion about whether or not you should relax your hair at home. Inquire about the condition of your hair to learn if it's healthy enough for home treatments.
- ask a friend to help you.
- read all directions and be sure you understand what to do at every step.
- be sure you have everything you need at your fingertips *before* you begin.
- protect scalp, forehead and ears with a petrolatum-based pomade.
- take the phone off the hook. Interruptions can cause you to lose track of the time, which may mean disaster for your hair.
- set a timer. Rinse the second the timer rings. Leaving the relaxer on too long causes *scarring alopecia*—a burned scalp—which can result in irreversible hair loss.
- shampoo thoroughly with the neutralizing shampoo. Use the entire bottle that comes with your relaxer kit to ensure that you have completely shampooed all the relaxer. Pay special attention to hard-to-reach areas—behind the ears, nape of neck.

WHEN IN DOUBT, DON'T

Timing is essential to properly relaxed hair. And it's important to be able to feel—and see—the degree to which the curl is being released. Obviously, this is more difficult to manage in the back than it is in the front.

Although the most wonderful aspect about hair is that it will grow back, when in doubt, *don't* relax at home.

In general, if you are good at shampooing, setting and styling your hair yourself, you probably will find it's easy to relax your own hair. But if you have two left hands and have trouble just pin curling your hair, you deserve the luxury of having your relaxing done by a pro.

TEXTURIZING

Texturizing is a partial relaxing technique which removes only some of the curl in curly hair. It's a favorite with Thaddeus Winston of Winston's on Melrose in Los Angeles.

Depending on the curly-wave pattern, Winston relaxes only enough to form waves or larger curls. By mixing a mild, sodium-hydroxide relaxer with oil he slows down the relaxing process. Hair is shampooed minutes after application, depending upon how naturally curly it is.

The result? More of the curl remains.

"Texturizing is a personal affair," Winston explains. "Your lifestyle and your hair's condition determine if removing just a degree of curl is right for you."

Texturizing is a wonderful solution for women who love water sports or who like to shampoo frequently. The curls and waves look similar to curly perms, but the hair is more natural-looking. In addition, there's no need for greasy oils and sprays to give hair artificial sheen and manageability.

MOISTURIZE AND RECONSTRUCT

Even though relaxers contain some conditioning ingredients, it's necessary to recondition every other time you shampoo. Moisturizers and reconstructors are high-powered conditioners which correct the moisture balance in relaxed hair.

"When hair is dry, most people think it needs oil," says La Fay of Simply Raw Salon in Los Angeles. "But when we are thirsty we don't drink oil, we drink water. Dry hair needs water—moisture—replaced in the hair shaft."

Combing, brushing and daily handling may cause tiny tears or breaks in the hair strand itself. Reconstructors fill in these areas so that hair has a smooth appearance and radiant texture.

"Reconstructing means you are replacing the cell structure deep within the cuticle. Hair has a natural sheen without oils," she explains.

La Fay offers these directions courtesy of Simply Raw.

Moisturizing Reconstructor for Relaxed Hair:

1. Shampoo hair with a pH-balanced shampoo; avoid balsam-type shampoos, which coat the hair shaft.
2. Using just a pea-size amount of Orr's Amino Acid Reconstructor, mix with a pea-size amount of Nexus Humectress Moisturizer.
    Note: Since this is highly concentrated you need only a tiny amount. When massaged between the palm of hands it "multiplies" and will be enough when applied to hair.
3. Wrap hair in a heat cap or plastic shower cap and sit under the dryer for fifteen minutes.

4. Because amino acids are highly concentrated, it may be necessary to shampoo hair gently following treatment. The reconstructor has penetrated the hair shaft, so what is rinsed away is only what has remained on the surface. The rest has penetrated into the cuticle.
5. Following shampoo, apply a "sealer" such as Sheen by Sebastian to close the cuticle and make hair easy to comb. A sealer also coats the hair shaft and protects it for blow-drying.

BLOW DRYING

Occasional use of a blow dryer, during travel or vacations, for instance, is time-saving. But constant use of blow dryers will dry and strip hair of natural oils so that hair looks dull.

If using a blow dryer is your preference, be sure to hold the dryer at least six inches from your hair. And keep the setting on medium—not hot.

Wet-setting hair, using plastic or metallic rollers and sitting under the dryer is still, in my opinion, one of the best ways to set relaxed hair. Curls last longer and the heat from a hooded dryer is less concentrated than the heat from a blow dryer.

Or, if you prefer having your hair set with a curling wand, try this: To minimize the amount of heat on your hair, after you shampoo gently comb hair and sit under a hooded dryer with the setting on cool or medium.

This step eliminates the need for a blow dryer and is easily adapted in the salon setting, too. It's great for hair that is baby-fine because the hooded dryer is similar to letting hair air-dry naturally.

Make sure hair and scalp are dry, but don't overdry hair. Set hair as usual with a medium-hot curling wand. Hair will have more thickness and body.

Now, enjoy the freedom of relaxed hair! Water sports and even getting caught in the rain may make your hair "frizzy," but your hair will not revert.

Remember, never press your hair with a hot comb once it's relaxed. But if pressing is your preference rather than relaxing, you'll find helpful information in the next chapter.

WARM-PRESSING

Thermal- or hot-comb-pressing has been modernized—no more smoky combs, no more heavy oils, no more hair that doesn't move. And since we've learned that our hair needs to be handled with care, the comb for pressing is not a *hot* one, but a *warm* one!

THE FRENCH CONNECTION

Pressing the hair to remove the curl has an interesting French connection. To help put a curl in European hair, Marcel Grateau invented the marcel iron in Paris in 1872.

The style was only temporary, since after curling, humidity caused European hair to become limp and straight. Still, it presented an attractive alternative for women and men who wanted to change looks between shampoos.

But before "marcels," or wavy hair, could become popular within our culture, another invention was needed first. And it took a woman to provide the solution.

America's first Black millionairess, Madame C. J. Walker, invented the metal pressing comb in 1901. Now the tight curliness of our hair could be released so that a larger curl could be styled with the marcel iron.

The effect was, and still is, temporary, lasting from shampoo to shampoo. Perspiration and humidity still cause hair to revert to its natural curly-wave pattern.

Your lifestyle determines how practical it is for you to warm-press your hair. A woman who swims daily, for instance, will find her lifestyle demands hair that requires less upkeep. Texturized hair or a natural may work better for the sports-active lifestyle.

But this inconvenience aside, pressed hair can be the answer to women who shy away from chemicals. It can also be a welcome alternative to women who are coping with excessive breakage or women who want to give their hair a rest from relaxers that were applied improperly.

With improved methods, pressed hair is still a popular—and preferred —option for thousands of Black women.

SCIENCE OF PRESSING

Mae Elliott has been styling hair for twenty-three years. She now sees only selected clients at the John Atchison Salon in Los Angeles. Mae believes thermal-pressed hair is very much in vogue because "pressing hair is natural to Black women. It's part of our heritage."

She has perfected the science of pressing and stresses that the comb should *never* be hot or smoky, only warm. Hair does not have to be pressed very straight because the curling wand applies more heat and will give hair the desired smooth texture. She advises unplugging the curling wand from time to time so that it doesn't become overheated.

Here are some additional tips from Mae Elliott for warm pressing your hair at home. Included in her steps is henna, because Mae feels it is an effective way to restore moisture to pressed hair. Henna does not have to be reapplied with every shampoo. Use only once every three months.

Note: Henna is *not* recommended for permanently relaxed hair because its effect on relaxed hair is less than ideal. In its effort to seal in moisture, henna will seal the outer layer, or *imbrications* "open" and hair will be coarse and hard to comb.

Mae Elliott's Directions for Warm-Pressing:

1. Shampoo hair once. Use a cleansing, pH-balanced shampoo. Avoid balsams because they coat the hair.
2. Blot hair dry with a towel. Do not rub towel against hair since this breaks hair and disturbs the scalp.
3. Mix Avigal Henna with boiling water until henna is a loose paste but not runny. Apply two teaspoons of vitamin E oil per cup of henna. Apply henna.
4. Wrap hair in a plastic cap.
5. Sit under a hooded dryer or wrap with a hot towel for forty-five minutes.
6. Shampoo once again with cleansing shampoo. Don't be concerned about any herbs that may be left in your hair. They will come out during drying and pressing.
7. Blot hair dry again.

8.   Dry hair using a blow dryer on medium setting. Hold the dryer four to six inches away from hair. Don't overdry hair, but be sure scalp is dry.

9.   Apply a tiny amount of lightweight oil to hair but never to scalp. Oil on the scalp clogs the pores and contributes to scalp burns when the oil gets hot from the heat of the comb. When pressing hair, be sure to use oil and not a cream hairdressing because creams contain water, which will cause hair to revert.

10.   With a warm comb, begin pressing hair away from the scalp at the *longest* end. Pressing hair closest to the scalp first pulls and breaks hair.

11.   Press hair in small sections for greater efficiency. Clip the rest of your hair out of the way with large metal clips.

12.   Once hair is pressed, use a warm curling wand to style hair. Be sure to unplug the wand occasionally so that it doesn't get too hot and singe hair.

One bonus of pressing is that if you decide to wear your hair naturally, all you have to do is shampoo. For the prettiest natural, see the next chapter.

TURNING HEADS

Top fashion and beauty model Peggy Dillard has recently opened her own salon in the heart of Harlem. As the proprietor of Turning Heads, located on 135th Street, Peggy caters to the woman who prefers to wear her hair beautiful, *naturally*.

MODELING THE NATURAL

As a model, Peggy Dillard prefers to be photographed wearing her hair styled in a natural.

"I find it to be more versatile," says Peggy who models for top designers both in the United States and in Europe. She explains why she initially made the transition from relaxed hair to natural hair.

"When I'm modeling, my hair is constantly set, combed and styled. All this handling made my relaxed hair overly dry and porous." For Peggy, natural hair provides more versatility, especially for her water sports.

"I love to swim! Although I prefer the beach, pools are the only choice when I'm in the city. Chlorine and daily shampooing did not mix well with my relaxed hair. So I came back to the natural because it works best for my active lifestyle."

VIRGIN TRAINING

When she decided to remove the chemical from her hair years ago, Peggy cut her hair so that it was only half an inch long. Although it allowed her to experiment with short hairstyles, more importantly she relearned how to work with her hair's natural texture.

"Growing hair from the shortest stage has wonderful advantages because virgin hair can be 'trained.' In addition, I've learned that my hair reacts differently in various temperatures and environments," says Peggy.

Photo of Peggy Dillard by Vince Frye

Braiding and twisting are excellent ways to wet-set natural hair. "Rather than being locked into one or two styles, I can set my hair wet for a looser look or twist it for a shorter, more tapered style." The result is a flattering, texturized style like the one Peggy models in these photographs.

"There are so many options to explore with our hair. When we dare to be creative, it demonstrates that we are secure with who we are."

Peggy shares some of her personal hair care tips, courtesy of Turning Heads.

Scalp Massage:

Scalp massage increases circulation by stimulating the sebaceous glands to produce more oil. Using the fleshy part of the fingertips, move the scalp upward, being careful not to move the hair against the scalp, but lifting the scalp over the cranium.

A once-a-week massage helps to redistribute natural oils. Brushing also removes exfoliated cells, but avoid excessive brushing, like one hundred strokes a night, which breaks fragile hair.

Shampoo:

Shampoo at least twice a week. Sometimes it may be necessary to shampoo more often to remove surface oil and debris, depending upon your environment.

Use mild herbal shampoos such as jojoba oil, camomile, walnut oil, rosewater or green apple. There are so many to choose from. But don't use any shampoo that strips or dries the hair. Make sure your herbal shampoo is pH-balanced.

Condition:

Because moisture escapes from the cuticle of curly hair, conditioning treatments are a healthy way to prevent hair from feeling—and looking—dry. With tight curls, sebum, the scalp's natural oil, does not easily reach the ends of hair. Conditioning gives shine and lustre where your hair needs it most.

Here is Peggy's *Four-Herb Deep-Oil Treatment* conditioner which cleanses and nourishes hair. The herbs she recommends may be purchased at most health food stores.

- Boil one tablespoon of sage, nettle, rosemary and burdock in two cups water. Even if you have only one or two of these herbs, this conditioner will still be effective. After boiling, let set five minutes. Strain, remove herbs; save the water from boiling.
- Mix three parts of the strained water with one part olive oil. Add juice of a lemon to help mix and stabilize ingredients. Let cool. Work into hair.
- Wrap hair with a warm towel for twenty minutes while you relax in a soothing tub with a good book. Shampoo. Rinse thoroughly.

Combing:

It's always best to comb natural hair while it is slightly damp. Even when it's dry, wet hair just a little before combing. If hair is very tangled, soften hair first by spritzing with a cream rinse.

Or, apply a tiny amount of almond oil or a lightweight hairdressing to wet hair but not to scalp.

Use a wide-tooth metal pick with thin prongs no more than one sixteenth of an inch in diameter. For long hair, use a pick with prongs that are at least four and a half inches long. A short pick will snap long hair.

Comb section by section rather than attempting to comb hair front to back in one sweep.

Cutting:

Cutting is essential to styling natural hair. Rather than patting your hair into the style you want, have a professional trim every six to eight weeks.

Freedom to wear your hair the way you want means you are comfortable with who you are. Whatever your choice, relaxed, pressed or natural hair allows you a great degree of versatility. Now, in the next section, experience the excitement of Color, Cut and Style!

Color, Cut, Style

ADD A LITTLE DRAMA

Black hair knows no limits, only luxurious styling options. The chapters in this section are designed for the woman who wants to add a little drama to her hair.

Splashes of color give new dimensions to any style. What type of haircolor works best for relaxed, pressed and natural hair? The answers are here.

With salons in New York and Los Angeles, John Atchison demonstrates that sculpted looks have the "Cutting Edge." Since women on the go demand quick, easy hairstyles, you'll find his workable suggestions for cuts that are as flexible as your schedule.

"Row upon Row" offers the prettiest cornrow look ever! Step-by-step how-tos include decorating with pearls for that special occasion.

Hairpieces and hair weaves can be wonderful additions for the woman who wants more. In "Hair Plus," there's up-to-date information for the latest technique in weaving.

And to add the perfect exclamation mark to this section, here's a peek into the "Fan-tasy!" of dazzling superstar singer Patti LaBelle. She talks about her hair attitude and tells why she dares to be so different.

With a little creativity, every woman can look—and be—her best. Here's to drama!

COLOR SPLASH

Monotoned color is a thing of the past. Splashes of color give light something wonderful to play with! Today's haircolor news surprises with fun-filled, face-framing accents. Hot spots of color at the nape of the neck or peaked near the crown allow you to be as creative and expressive as your mood. The only limit is your imagination!

EITHER/OR

Black women no longer have to play the "either/or" game—either relaxer or color, but not both. Now, we can enjoy the best of two worlds with shimmering semipermanent shades that actually make chemically treated hair look healthier.

Women who prefer pressed hair or naturals can enjoy the full-range of haircoloring options from semipermanent color to permanent haircolor. What works best for your hair?

ONLY TEMPORARY

Temporary color lasts only from shampoo to shampoo. These are the colors which are the most fun, because for that party or special occasion you can experiment with the boldest color statement. Shampoo it away if you decide it's not you.

New forms of temporary color are always sprouting, but the most popular are color mousses. That means that in addition to a styling help, you'll get a color boost!

Because alcohol makes hair dry and brittle, select mousses that are alcohol-free.

SEMIPERMANENT

Since they are minus peroxide or ammonia—hazardous for women with relaxed hair—semipermanent color is safe and gentle. Color glazes each strand so hair looks thicker, richer and fuller with healthy shine. It's like body-building for your hair!

Semipermanent color rinses away little by little and lasts from four to six shampoos. There's never a need for retouching because the color gradually fades with every shampoo. Hair cannot be dramatically lightened with semipermanent color, but you can darken hair or cover the gray without changing your natural haircolor.

Another term for semipermanent haircolor is *shampoo-in haircolor* because it's applied to dry hair just before you shampoo. What works even better, however, is to shampoo hair *first* as you would normally and let it partially air-dry. *Then* apply semipermanent color to clean, slightly damp hair for more vibrant color that lasts longer.

Apply semipermanent color to roots first, then to ends of hair. If you relax, color the week or two following your relaxer.

Sitting under a hooded dryer for twenty minutes after the color has been applied intensifies results. Then rinse, rinse, rinse.

Another type of semipermanent color is *cellophane.* Like a thin coat of translucent color over polished nails, the name cellophane describes the subtle effect of glimmering color which adds sheer tones to your hair.

Fuchsia, wine, raspberry, blueberry, black orchid, red cherry and violet are some of cellophane's vibrant shades. Because the color is *so* transparent, cellophane is not a terrific way to cover the gray.

Some women find that their hair feels dry with a cellophane. Be prepared to condition more often.

IT'S PERMANENT

It won't shampoo out. It won't fade. It will lighten hair. It will darken and cover the gray. It's permanent haircolor. But it's not for everyone.

Primarily, the benefits of permanent haircolor are limited to women who have virgin hair or who warm-press their hair. A few women who relax might have good results with permanent haircolor, but for most, the mixture of peroxide or ammonia and the relaxer proves to be too much for fragile hair. Breakage right down to the roots often results.

Because two processes are involved—first removing existing color, then applying a new color—permanent color is best done in the salon. And this is where the expertise of the hairstylist is most valuable.

A professional can determine whether or not permanent color is right for you and help you select the perfect shade for your skin tone. Once you have success with salon permanent color, then you can experiment with permanent haircolor at home.

Even though the product says "shampoo-in permanent haircolor," remember it still contains strong chemicals to first bleach, then dye your hair.

If you have a relaxer and insist on permanent color, have color applied *only* professionally and wait at least three or four weeks after your touch-up.

Always insist on a strand test. Color a tiny section of hair behind the ear and wait four to six weeks to see how hair reacts. If all is well, color away! Since color is permanent, when in doubt choose the lighter shade. Permanent color requires a commitment, because roots must be retouched every six to eight weeks.

Some women have allergic reactions, called *contact dermatitis,* and experience general malaise, pimples or a balloonlike swelling in the face. If you have any negative reaction, see your dermatologist *immediately.*

COLOR ROBBERS

Once you use color, whether it's temporary, semipermanent or permanent, you'll want to enjoy sports other than swimming, at least for the first week or so.

Semipermanent color only coats the hair shaft and will trickle down your face to your bathing suit if your hair becomes wet. A snug-fitting swim cap offers some protection.

In general, remember sun and chlorine are the biggest color robbers. Protect hair with a regular deep-conditioning treatment weekly and wear a scarf or wide-brimmed hat prior to sunning.

THE CUTTING EDGE

From New York to Los Angeles, hairstylists are giving Black women the cutting edge. Bold cuts and bolder shapes extend the boundaries of hair. Whether it's freestyle or softly set, it's simply fabulous!

PRECISION CUTTING

Master cutter John Atchison, who apprenticed with Vidal Sassoon, sets the pace in precision cutting. He has salons in New York and Los Angeles, and his clients include the full range of active women—housewives, secretaries, business and professional women, students, models, actresses, singers.

"The right haircut frees up valuable time," says John. "Hair requires less home maintenance because the shape is already in the cut."

It's not enough that hair performs well and looks great in the salon. "Just as a good dress is a good dress without adding jewelry, the right haircut should make a statement of its own without reliance upon rollers, sprays or mousses. All it should take is pin curls at night or a quick morning set for hair to fall into place."

The haircut, says John, is what remains after all else has been removed.

IT'S INDIVIDUAL

The challenge for the stylist is to design a look which is individual and distinctive. Above all, the cut should be flattering to height, weight, figure and features.

A geometric cut, one that holds a shape you can wear without being roller-set, is what a busy lifestyle demands.

This flexibility means that hair can be simply shampooed and left to dry naturally. Or, for a softer, smoother effect, hair can be curled. The photos in this chapter are excellent examples of the freedom this type of haircut offers.

Photo: George Selman. Makeup: Rudy Calvo. Hair: John Atchison

CUTTING FOR LENGTH

Cutting hair regularly when you are growing for length seems like a contradiction in terms. But it's not.

"Hair is fuller and doesn't snag and break when dead ends are trimmed regularly," says John. "It's important to have a professional trim every two months if you want length."

Since hair farthest from the scalp is the oldest, it has been shampooed and curled the most. Damage usually appears at the ends first. Split ends can stunt hair growth because they snag and get caught in the comb or brush, causing hair to break. Luster and shine are lost because of dull, frizzy ends.

As Black women, we are particularly sensitive about the scissors. Because curly hair takes longer to grow, it takes more time for our hair to reach the length we want. Unfortunately, some stylists don't "hear" when the request is only for a trim. Instead, a drastic cut, much to our surprise, means starting all over again.

Photo: George Selman. Makeup: Rudy Calvo. Hair: John Atchison

However, nothing looks as polished as hair that is properly shaped, so the solution is not to avoid the scissors altogether. Find a stylist who understands your needs and who trims without cutting if that's what you want. Once you have confidence you'll probably be ready—and happy—to try any suggestion.

If your hair has been cut too short, don't despair. Remind yourself that it's only temporary and try to experiment with your "new" look.

GROWING LAYERED CUTS

Are you ready for a change and want your hair all one length? Here is John's suggestion for growing out a layered cut.

Have the longest sections trimmed regularly to keep them at one length. Don't trim the shorter sections, but allow them to catch up to the longer hair. Once the layered sections are even, hair can grow uniformly to the full length you desire.

SHORT CUTS

To maintain short cuts, John suggests a trim every four to six weeks to redefine the shape of your style. If hair grows quickly or if your haircut is one that demands precision, you may find it necessary to have a trim more often, like every two weeks.

How do you know when you are ready for a trim? Once you have to push or pat your hair into the shape you want, it's time to give ends a snip. The time you spend styling your hair will be cut in half when the cut holds its own.

FINANCING THE CUT

A good haircut is a financial investment. But isn't it a wonderful feeling when your hair looks just right?

You don't mind tipping the stylist 10 to 15 percent of your bill when you've had undivided attention and are pleased with the way you look. No matter how excited you are, though, remember that if the proprietor of the salon cuts your hair, tipping is appreciated, but it's optional.

Like a renewed relationship, the right haircut makes you fall in love with your hair all over again. Is it time for a little romance in *your* life?

ROW UPON ROW

Cornrows are a convenient way to style hair for the prettiest ethnic statement. A creative blend of patterns, adorned with decorative pearls or colorful beads, can transform any look from daytime to wedding!

HOW TO CORNROW

New York stylist Sonia Bullock designed this style for *Bride's* magazine. Because cornrows are long-lasting and trouble-free, they are a wonderful solution to traveling times, like the honeymoon, when the last thing you want to worry about is your hair.

Below, Sonia explains how to cornrow and decorate your hair. Her tips are designed to transform you into the most stunning—and carefree—bride!

- Set aside five hours to have your hair braided a day before your wedding. Shampoo and condition. Let hair dry naturally. To remove excess moisture, use a blow dryer with the setting on cool. Remember to hold the dryer at least six inches from hair.
- Once hair is completely dry, comb, then brush hair back and off face and neck high into a ponytail that's loosely secured at the crown. As you cornrow, you will angle the rows back and upward, toward the center of your head, so that each cornrow meets at the crown in a ponytail.
- Starting at the top center, loosen and part hair to form a small row that goes straight back from the middle of your forehead to the crown. Now cornrow hair, weaving in strands from the scalp so that the cornrow lies as flat as possible. When you reach the crown area, continue braiding an individual braid for the length of the hair hank. Secure the end of this braid with a bobby pin.
- Continue in even sections and angle the cornrows so that they

Photo: Ishimuro for **Bride's** *magazine* © *Condé Nast Publications, Inc.*

spiral toward the crown. Once you're complete, remove bobby pins and gather ends; twist hair into a topknot and use hairpins to secure.

- To sleep, wear a silk or nylon scarf to keep the cornrows neat. Pearls are added the morning of the wedding.
- On wedding morning, set aside at least two hours. Thread a sewing needle with black thread or thread to match the color of your hair; knot. Sewing away from your forehead, glide the needle into the center cornrow. Anchor the knot right at the tip of the cornrow.
- Glide three pearls or colorful beads onto the needle. Now, working backward, toward the crown, weave the needle in and secure pearls by making a knot; cut thread.
- Repeat for the rows on either side of the center. This time, leave an inch between each grouping and continue adding pearls until you reach the crown area. Knot and cut thread.
- Continue sewing pearls in the pattern as pictured, beading every fifth row. Or create a design of your own!
- To remove, carefully lift thread, cut, pull out pearls.

HOW TO SHAMPOO

This style can last for up to two weeks, so you'll want to shampoo every four or five days without undoing your cornrows. Here's how:

- Suds shampoo into the palms of your hands and gently massage it into your hair and scalp. Use only the fleshy part of your fingertips so that you do not scratch the exposed scalp.
- Rinse by gently running water over your hair. You may find this easier in the shower. Wrap head with a towel to blot excess water.
- Tie hair with a soft fabric scarf to "set" cornrows flat again. Allow hair to dry naturally.

TAUT IS TOO TIGHT

Although you want your cornrows to last, tight braiding is not the way to ensure longevity. If hair is pulled taut so that it has no give or slack, it's too tight.

In addition to damaging the hair strand, tight braiding pulls the fine *lanugo* hairs right out of the edges of the hairline. Hair loss, which dermatologists call *traction alopecia,* also occurs in between the rows.

If cornrows are worn for too long, traction alopecia can look like a receding hairline. The longer cornrows are worn, the more the hairline will recede. Hair grows back over a period of time when the cornrows are removed, but if they are worn too long, this hairloss can be permanent.

BY THE ROOTS

Many women feel that their hair grows faster when it's cornrowed or braided. Actually, it only *appears* to grow faster because when braiding is undone, the normal day-to-day growth is seen all at once.

Pulling hair tightly on the surface of the scalp is not going to encourage the roots of hair below the scalp to work any faster. It just pulls hair out by the roots.

Short-term wear is ideal for this stunning style. If your face and figure are proportioned to balance this look, you are what the world views to be the epitome of a beautiful Black woman.

HAIR PLUS!

Full, fuller, fullest! Our love affair with hair has us going to all lengths. We can blend falls right into our own hair or completely weave for maximum volume. Best of all, there's nothing telltale. Your hairdresser is the *only* one who has to know for sure!

PIECING IT TOGETHER

Switches, chignons, braids and falls are hairpieces that bring versatility to any hairstyle. A switch added to the front or back of hair gives a longer dimension to a very short haircut. Chignons and braids pinned to pulled-back hair are elegant for evening. A fall blended right into shorter hair creates a few extra waves.

"The woman who wants to change her look, yet still wear her natural hair, has so many choices available to her," says California-based André Weeks of It's a Wig, owned by his brother, Michael Weeks.

"And because hairpieces are designed to match the texture of Black women's hair, the result is totally flattering."

Hairpieces today are very comfortable to wear. Intelligent construction makes them natural-looking and lightweight, a perfect addition to any hair wardrobe.

This practical advice from André may come in handy. "Just as every woman should have at least one wig in her hair accessories, she should also have one hairpiece. When she wants to add a special touch to her hairstyle, she'll have the perfect solution at her fingertips."

WEAVING IN MORE

Hair weaving, temporarily adding human hair right into your own hair,

Photo: George Selman

is another option for Black women. Though not inexpensive, weaving can last from three to six months, depending on your lifestyle.

"A hair weave can make anyone's dream come true," says Afua Asiedu, a private hair designer in Los Angeles.

"Hair has a chance to 'rest' and is free from daily manipulation or excessive heat from blow dryers. Entertainers especially realize these benefits, especially when their hair is protected from hot lights."

Singer Lola Falana, actress Sheryl Lee Ralph and renowned trumpeter Miles Davis are among the stars who have sported styles by Afua.

TWO WAYS TO WEAVE

Weaving can be done two ways—with needle and thread or by braiding. Although the former is a popular method of weaving hair, braided extensions are the newest way to hair weave.

Using 100 percent human hair, extensions are braided from the scalp into individual braids that are about one eighth to one fourth of an inch long.

"Hair is then combed to camouflage the braids so that it looks completely natural," says Afua. "And the bonus is that hair has motion!"

Braiding, which should never be done too tightly, can take anywhere from eight to twenty-four hours to complete. Since the hair is not braided directly onto the scalp, shampooing is easy.

Best of all, hair weaves are not limited to the rich and famous. Any woman who wants lots of hair to fling over her shoulders can have as much as she wants!

FAN-TASY!

Superstar Patti LaBelle is a woman who lives her fan-tasy! If the mood hits, she adds pieces to her hair in unusual designs. Patti is so creative that she is always changing her hairstyle. But because they are so unique, the focus here is on those incredible fans!

PATTI LABELLE

Like everything else she does, Patti LaBelle puts her heart-filled energy into her crowning glory—her hair. When she sings a song, it's no longer ordinary. And when she experiments with hair design, it's . . . well . . . extraordinary!

"My hair attitude can be described in one word: *freedom!*" says Patti. "That means a hairstyle is as flexible as my mood. Since I don't feel the same way all the time, why should I always wear my hair the same?"

Patti feels true freedom is the ability to be open, to be flexible and expressive. "Working with my hair is one way that makes me feel different and look beautiful. I want to feel—and I do!—that I can do anything with my hair whether regal and sophisticated, cute and fluffy, or, sometimes, completely outrageous."

To demonstrate her belief in versatility, Patti never wears the same hair design twice. Every time she appears onstage, it's with a look that's created especially for that moment.

"There are so many dimensions to beauty. Why should I limit myself with just one look?" she asks. "I change my dress, my shoes, my makeup. What about my hair?"

And, asks Patti, "Why only work with the hair that's rooted in my head? My hair designer, Norma Harris, and I love to experiment. We use pieces, switches and fans to get a unique look."

PATTI'S HAIR DESIGNER

Norma Harris, who has traveled with Patti LaBelle for years personally creating each fan-tasy, considers herself a hair designer rather than a hair-stylist.

Photo of Patti LaBelle by Marc Raboy. Makeup: Rudy Calvo

"I don't *do* hair. I *sculpt* hair," explains Norma. "I don't curl, perm or straighten. My trademark is cutting and sculpture."

Every design Patti wears is unique, an image sculpted just for her. "Artists should always create different styles. When we use imagination, there isn't a need to copy each other. I agree with Patti when she says that her hair attitude is freedom—freedom for the designer, and freedom for the woman wearing the design."

FANS

The look they are both most proud of is the fans. "We wanted to do something really different, and something really Patti. The fans offer a bit of a surprise and a lot of variety," explains Norma.

By combing Patti's hair into the fans and spraying hair and hairpiece together, images are sculpted from tulips, leaves, crowns, a bird's wing.

"I even sculpted a bucket for a television special and had her own hair falling out of the bucket," laughs Norma. "And for the Statue of Liberty Celebration Concert, Patti wore Liberty Fans!"

To create each design, Norma first sketches her image on paper, using sharp lines and geometric angles.

"I then cut human hair into these shapes to make fans. Next, the fans are added to Patti's hair and I comb and press both fans and hair together. I'd rather use the fans than Patti's own hair because I don't want to damage her hair. Finally, I spray the fans—my little secret—and secure them with a few bobby pins. It takes about forty-five minutes."

Patti would not be able to perform as freely as she does were these fans cumbersome. "They are very lightweight and easy to wear," explains her stylist. "To remove the fans, I apply plenty of conditioner."

YOU DON'T HAVE TO BE A STAR

Patti reminds us that you don't have to be a star to enjoy the unbridled freedom of honest self-expression.

"My one suggestion is this: Be open! Experiment! Try looks that are bolder, styles that are a bit more daring."

She adds, "And once in a while, enter a new dimension—a style only *you* could dream of. You'll never know if it can work for you unless you are courageous enough to be different. You may surprise yourself and find you are freer in your mind than you ever imagined!"

Skin News

YOU LOOK MARVELOUS!

If there's one major lesson we've learned in the beauty world it's this: beautiful skin is no mistake.

The complex organ we call skin actually mirrors the health of our internal organs. When properly nourished inside with the right foods and stimulated by daily exercise, and when renewed and refreshed outside with an intelligently tailored skin-care regimen, you can't help but look marvelous!

Black women have the edge on "Lovely Complexions." The reason is the pigment melanin, which gives black skin its color. How to keep our complexions lovely and prevent dark marks, and how to remove facial and body hairs are some of the topics discussed here.

"Preparing the Canvas" offers a daily skin-care regimen for your specific skin type. Along with tips, there's an easy-to-follow chart with product suggestions from dermatologist Darlene D. Sampson, M.D.

On the pampering side, "Steam, Sauna and Spa" not only feel good, they are good. For the best results, the how-tos are here.

John A. Kenney, Jr., M.D., explains why black skin has special concerns. James W. Hobbs, M.D., tells how to cope with acne, and Pearl E. Grimes, M.D., spotlights important breakthroughs in the treatment of vitiligo in "Cosmetic Challenges."

There are also special considerations when it comes to cosmetic surgery. In "Aesthetic Appeal," dermatologist Harold E. Pierce, M.D., discusses the right motives for changing facial features. And A. Paul Kelly, M.D., tells how to correct earlobe scars which result from piercing.

Healthy skin—it's not to be taken for granted. With the right information and a little care, you can make the most of a good thing!

Photo: Bill King. Courtesy Vogue, *October 1986. Copyright © Condé Nast Publications, Inc.*

LOVELY COMPLEXIONS

Black women are known for having lovely complexions—ageless . . . rich . . . beautiful.

POWERFUL PIGMENT

Melanin is pigment which gives brown skin its color. It's powerful, because it literally blocks the sun's harmful rays from penetrating beneath the skin's surface.

Since wrinkling occurs when elastic tissues are destroyed by ultraviolet rays, sunshine can be the skin's worst enemy. The more exposure there is, the more wrinkling is likely to occur.

Black women often look years younger because the darker the complexion, the more melanin there is. That means added protection from wrinkling. What a blessing!

But, that does not mean we don't need any protection at all from the sun. Our skin tans—and burns—so wearing sunscreen during bathing and boating is a must.

NOT OILIER

Oil and sweat glands lubricate and cool the skin. According to John A. Kenney, Jr., M.D., professor of dermatology, Howard University College of Medicine, many people incorrectly believe that black skin is oilier than others and that's why it stays younger-looking longer. Not true.

Light reflected from dark skin, or any dark surface, makes it appear shiny, but shine does not mean the complexion is oily. Dr. Kenney explains that black skins do not have more *sebaceous,* or oil, glands. Neither are there more *sudoriferous,* or sweat, glands. And no, it's not "thicker," either.

But there are bigger *melanosomes*—pigment cells. Melanin helps skin heal. In black skins, too much melanin often rushes to the rescue, causing dark marks, called *hyperpigmentation.*

"Irritation, sunburn, abrasion, or inflammation from a pimple stimulates melanocytes," Dr. Kenney explains. "Once these cells become stimulated, they produce more pigmentation than the surrounding melanocytes and a dark mark results."

DARK MARKS

Simply squeezing a pimple or scrubbing too harshly can cause a dark mark which can take days, weeks, sometimes months to clear. For this reason, it's important to seek the help of a qualified esthetician, especially if you have problem skin.

At Skinn by Nathalie in Los Angeles, the face is gently cleansed, then pampered with a soothing fifteen-minute steam before the extraction of pimples. Afterwards, skin is renourished and a mask applied to tone and seal.

"Skin must be properly prepared before it can be extracted," explains Nathalie. "Abruptly picking the face is what causes dark marks."

Cosmetic allergies or reactions to medications, such as the birth-control pill, may also cause hyperpigmentation.

If a dark mark persists, an over-the-counter cream containing 2 percent *hydroquinone,* which is a safe skin bleach, effectively slows down the rate at which melanocytes produce melanosomes. This allows skin to return to its normal color. Skin lighteners will not make you lighter than your original color, but are an effective way to clear any discolorations.

To even your complexion and remove the darkening that occurs from years of sun exposure, apply a skin lightener cream to both face and neck. Use once in the morning and once at night until the complexion clears. Expect to wait three weeks for the lightener to work, then apply only at bedtime.

With skin lighteners, a mild irritation—temporary redness or darkening —is considered to be normal. However, if irritation becomes severe, stop use and see a dermatologist. Never, *never* apply this cream under or around the eyes or on any broken or inflamed skin.

When using any product which contains hydroquinone, limit sun exposure. Since ultraviolet light stimulates pigment cells, it's recommended to apply sunscreen when going outdoors. A better idea is to select a skin cream which already contains sunscreen.

While skin-lighteners which are available without a prescription can clear minor hyperpigmentation, more serious skin discolorations require the expertise of a dermatologist who is familiar with our skin. A cream with a higher amount of hydroquinone, as much as 10 percent, can be prescribed.

FACIAL GESTURES

Facial gestures are an easy way to induce wrinkles. Constant frowning causes deep furrows along the brow area. Squinting encourages crow's-feet to leave their print on delicate eye tissues.

Bad habits, too, can age your face faster than the damaging rays of the sun. Smoking cigarettes not only causes halitosis, it also carves lines around the mouth. And chewing gum—the most unladylike of all habits—besides not being chic, stretches and sags skin at the cheeks.

In general, any motion that stretches, tugs or pulls skin, like leaning your face into hands for a headrest, is a no-no. Facial exercises are the exception. They encourage the release of tension so that your face is more relaxed.

When applying cosmetics, always think "upward, outward," to work against the pull of gravity. In the area right underneath the eyes, use the pinky finger to apply moisturizers and foundation with small, patting motions, working inward, toward the bridge of the nose, to discourage lines.

FACIAL HAIRS

Some women consider facial hairs to be rather appealing. To others, excessive hair around the sides of the face, above the lip or around the chin, is annoying.

There are several ways to remove these hairs, but which way is safest for our skin? Since dark complexions hyperpigment easily, the best method of hair removal must be one that does not leave any telltale spots behind.

If there are just a few stray hairs, *tweezing* is the easiest way to remove them. First, cleanse the area with a cotton ball soaked in astringent. A splash of cold water or a bit of ice after tweezing will reduce any stinging or swelling.

Shaving, to remove either stray eyebrow hairs or hair around the lip area, is a hair-removal method to be done with care. Moisten the skin with cream or soap before you begin. Although quick and easy, shaving is not very effective. Hair grows back quickly and the stubby regrowth at the skin's surface is obvious. Tweezing the eyebrows is a better solution, and for above the lip, waxing gives better, longer-lasting results.

Waxing, though not exactly painless, is an efficient way of hair removal and can be done right in the skin-care salon where you have your facial. A thin layer of warm melted wax is spread over the area where hair is to be removed. When the wax is pulled off, the hairs come out from below the skin's surface, at the root, so there's no stubble. It takes several weeks for hair to reappear, but when it does, it grows in finer than before and, eventually, hair regrowth is minimal. For best results, allow at least two weeks of hair growth before you wax.

Depilatories work by softening and dissolving hairs so that they can be wiped away. Creams, lotions and foams are applied for approximately fifteen minutes before hair removal is complete. Depilatories also discourage hair regrowth and hair grows back less noticeably. Follow directions carefully and do a patch test first by applying the depilatory to a small area.

Permanent methods of hair removal include *depilatron* and *electrolysis.* Both require a series of repeated treatments and the number depends upon hair growth. With depilatron, an electronic tweezer sends heat currents deep into the hair follicle where hair grows. Once the root is sterilized, hair does not grow again. This procedure is reportedly painless.

Electrolysis, on the other hand, is often painful. A needle, inserted into the hair follicle, sends sharp electrical currents to the hair root. This method of hair removal is not recommended for black skin because it can leave hyperpigmentation.

A newer procedure, *thermolysis,* generates heat only at the tip of the needle, preventing hyperpigmentation and scarring.

It works like this: A Teflon-coated needle with a bare tip is inserted into the hair follicle with a gentle, delicate touch. Then, a burst of heat is sent to the root of the hair follicle, but it is not felt along the entire hair shaft. Reportedly, there's a feeling of warmth, but not pain.

Dr. Harold E. Pierce in Bala Cynwyd, Pennsylvania, is successfully using thermolysis with his Black patients.

To minimize facial hair without actual removal, *bleaching* offers an effective camouflage. Use a product specifically designed for the face and bleach hair in stages. If you try to lighten hair all at once, you may make it too light and end up with a blond mustache! Instead, bleach the color a little at a time, then bleach a little more the next day.

In the next chapter, your daily skin-care regimen is outlined by a leading Black dermatologist.

PREPARING THE CANVAS

Just as the artist prepares the surface of the canvas before creating a master-piece, so, too, do we prepare our skin before adding even the sheerest color. A daily cleansing regimen using the right products gives us skin that is gloriously healthy.

BARE FACES

Our cleansing regimen is so important that it should be adhered to with religious zeal. And because the modern word in makeup is "minimal," we must pay closer attention to our complexions so we can confidently bare our faces to the world.

There are very few of us, if any, who can boast of perfect complexions all the time. Genetics has a lot to do with how prone we are to breakouts, or how quickly we age. Still, we cannot minimize the importance of proper skin-care treatments mingled with a professional facial at least three to six times a year.

Beauty experts believe that taking care of your skin while you are young, then adapting your regimen as you mature, is paramount. Since your internal health and lifestyle are mirrored outside, this regimen includes eating right and getting an adequate amount of beauty sleep.

Just as it's impossible to separate your skin from you, so, too, is it impossible to separate a healthy approach to feeling—and looking—your absolute best.

Then, being knowledgeable about products and their ingredients is the formula which guarantees that you are making intelligent beauty choices.

HARSH PRODUCTS

Darlene D. Sampson, M.D., diplomate of the American Board of Dermatology and in private practice with offices in Inglewood, Manhattan Beach and Los Angeles, California, says, "Black women sometimes use products that are too harsh for their skin, because they mistakenly believe their skin is oily."

Soaps which dry and strip needed oils from the skin often leave irritation and patchy areas. These areas are further aggravated by harsh alcohol or astringents that are too strong.

"Alcohol is too harsh for anyone," advises Dr. Sampson. "It will even dry an oily complexion."

In addition to soaps, moisturizers can also cause irritation, roughness and tiny bumps. She cautions that women should avoid applying vitamin E oil to their skin.

"If a sensitivity develops and there is sun exposure, the result can be quite devastating. An extreme sunburn, or *photodermatitis,* can result even in Black patients."

Dr. Sampson's list of other ingredients to avoid includes: lanolin, myristate, DNC red dyes, stearic acids, laureth 4, neopentanoate and palmitate.

IN THE BAG

Knowing your skin type is the best assurance that you are following the correct cleansing regimen. Using a swatch from a brown paper bag, says Dr. Sampson, is the best way to determine whether your skin is normal, dry, oily or combination.

After cleansing your face in the morning as you would normally, do not apply any moisturizer. By noon, you're ready for this paper test.

From a brown paper bag, cut out two four-by-four-inch squares, one for each cheek, and one four-by-eight-inch length for the T-zone—forehead, nose, chin.

Press each square firmly against cheek so that it will absorb any oil. Notice how it comes away from your skin. Does it stick? Now, hold the square up to the light and examine. Are there stains?

Press the longer piece of paper down the middle of your face, concentrating on forehead, nose and chin. Once again, notice how it comes away from your skin and hold it up to the light and examine.

IT'S NORMAL

In the normal complexion, the square will not have any stains and it comes away from the face fairly easily. When you look at your skin closely, you'll notice it has a fresh appearance.

IT'S DRY

Dry skin has a flaky appearance and the square doesn't "stick" to the face at all. There are no oil stains from the T-zone, either. Extremely dry skin may even be scaly or cracked.

IT'S OILY

If oil noticeably stains the bag, you have oily skin. Your skin looks as if it needs another cleansing, and when you run your fingers across your face your skin will feel slippery. Pores may be enlarged on cheeks, chin, nose and forehead.

IT'S COMBINATION

Combination skin is so called because there are two types of complexions: normal and oily. The squares from the cheeks may not have any stains, yet the patch for the T-zone is quite oily. Also, when you look closely, pores in this area may be slightly enlarged.

Rather than having dry, normal or oily skin, most women actually have combination. Special attention to the T-zone will balance the complexion, minimizing excess oils.

CLEANSING CHART

The chart below makes cleansing your normal, dry, oily or combination skin easy! Dr. Sampson has outlined this daily regimen and offers a suggestion of products she feels are gentle enough to cleanse even the most delicate face.

NORMAL

A.M.	Cleanse, using a fresh washcloth or gentle buff puff. Rinse with warm water, then cool. Pat dry. Apply a light, water-based moisturizer.
P.M.	In the evening, cleanse face as in A.M. With cotton balls, apply a toner to remove any traces of soil until cotton comes away from face clean. Apply moisturizer.
Soaps	Nutura Creamy Wash Off Cleanser by Avon, Neutrogena

Original Formula, Dove, Camay for Normal Skin, Purpose Soap.

Moisturizers   Nutura Light Replenishing Lotion by Avon, Neutrogena Moisture, Formula 405 Light Texture.

P.S.   Normal skin demands little attention. Anything goes! But don't take your complexion for granted. Be consistent and follow a sensible regimen daily.

DRY

A.M.   Cleanse face gently, using only a fresh washcloth. Or use cotton rolled in paper towel which is not too abrasive for your skin. Discard after use. Rinse with warm, then cool water. Pat skin dry but only enough to remove excess water. With face damp, apply an emollient moisturizer.

P.M.   In the evening, cleanse as in A.M. Or, you may prefer a creamy cleanser such as cold cream. Apply toner diluted with water to remove excess soil with fresh cotton balls until the last comes away from face clean. Apply moisturizer to slightly damp face, paying special attention to particularly dry areas.

Soaps   Accolade Complete Cleansing Complex by Avon, Neutrogena for Dry Skin, Dove, Basis, Purpose Soap.

Moisturizers   Avon's Accolade Daytime Moisture Support and Night Treatment, Neutrogena Moisture, Formula 405 Regular Moisturizer.

P.S.   Avoid substances that are going to further dry out your complexion, like alcohol or benzoyl peroxide. Cold, dry climates may irritate skin further, causing it to itch, flake, crack. A humidifier adds moisture to the air which can be absorbed by your sensitive skin. During the daytime, spritz face with purified mineral water to restore moisture. Apply additional moisturizer as needed.

Eczema, or atopic dermatitis, is caused by skin hypersensitivity to unknown compounds. It's called "the itch that rashes," because itching precedes the rash. Seek professional help. Your dermatologist can prescribe topical corticosteroids to relieve skin discomfort.

OILY

A.M.   Use either the gentle or the regular buff puff, but be careful you're not too abrasive in an effort to really clean your skin. You could irritate instead. Rinse with warm, then cool water. Apply a light-textured moisturizer if needed.

P.M.   In the evening, cleanse as in A.M. Using cotton balls and an astringent which contains a small amount of diluted alcohol, remove excess soil and oil until cotton comes away from face clean. If skin is especially oily, you probably do not need to apply a moisturizer.

Soaps   Avon's Clearskin 2 Anti-Bacterial Cleansing Cake, Neutrogena Oily Formula, Neutrogena Acne Cleansing Formula, Acnaveen, Sastid.

Moisturizers   Avon's Clearskin 2 Oil-Free Moisture Supplement, Formula 405 Light Texture Moisturizer.

P.S.   Too much scrubbing can further stimulate overactive oil glands—the result, face is not cleaner, but actually oilier! Soaps containing sulfur are especially beneficial to oily skin. However, if you are acne-prone, do not try to remedy your complexion problem yourself. Seek professional help to prevent dark marks. A discussion of acne is in the chapter "Cosmetic Challenges."

COMBINATION

A.M.   Cleanse face with fresh washcloth. Rinse with warm, then cool water. Apply moisturizer all over face.

P.M.   In the evening, again cleanse as in A.M. Apply a toner with cotton balls until cotton comes away from face clean. Moisturize dry areas, cheeks, only, but not forehead, nose, chin.

Soaps   Avon's Pure Care Purifying Gentle Cleanser, Neutrogena Original Formula, Dove.

Moisturizers   Avon's Pure Care Moisture Shield, Neutrogena Moisture, Formula 405 Light Texture.

P.S.   It's important to use the right soap, one that's not too drying for dry areas and not too oily for oily areas. During the day as needed, blot forehead, cheek and chin with a tissue to remove excess oil.

BODY CARE

Oil glands help hold moisture in the skin. Since they are clustered in the center of the face, upper and midback, and V of the chest where the blouse opens, the remainder of the trunk and extremities often tend to be dry.

Dr. Sampson recommends these lubricating lotions which provide an occlusive barrier to hold water in the skin to prevent skin from cracking and flaking: Neutrogena Sesame Seed Formula, Lubriderm, Keri Lotion.

An additional help for dry skin is a quick soak in a warm tub with Avon's Skin-So-Soft. After bathing, pat skin until it's just moist, then apply lotion.

If skin is particularly dry, try to avoid air conditioning, which removes needed moisture from the air.

For more body tips, see the next chapter, "Steam, Sauna and Spa."

STEAM, SAUNA AND SPA

Beautiful skin—it's great to be inside of, wonderful to look at and a pleasure to touch. Knowing how to effectively use steam and sauna to cleanse and seal in moisture, the youth potion of your skin, will keep face and body supple!

CAL-A-VIE

Nestled along the scenic coastline just north of San Diego is this newest spa, Cal-A-Vie, in Vista, California.

Resembling a remote European village, this spa offers the best in beauty and aromatherapy treatments. Its quaint villas and rock-piled hot springs are punctuated everywhere with fragrant sprays of lavender and naturally grown herbs.

Spa director Susan Power believes herbs are a natural way to stimulate the body and detoxify the system.

"Through gentle vaporizing action, skin is encouraged to perspire to cleanse pores. Aromatherapy, the use of plants, herbs and flowers for beauty treatments, is a luxurious way to refresh, revitalize."

CHAMOMILE

The medicinal properties in the scented foliage and flower heads of chamomile give a gentle, aromatherapeutic facial massage. Kim Ulen, head esthetician at Cal-A-Vie, tells how to steam your face properly using a mild blend of chamomile tea.

A gentle steam for normal, dry or oily skin:
- Let herbs set in just-boiled water—removed from the stove—approximately five minutes. This allows water to cool sufficiently so it's not too hot.

- While chamomile steams, mix two teaspoons of uncooked oatmeal, one tablespoon ground almonds, one tablespoon milk and one-half teaspoon honey for a honey-almond facial scrub. Set aside.
- Wrap hair in a towel. Cleanse face, first removing eye makeup with mineral oil, then removing oil residue with cotton and warm water. Rinse entire face with warm water.
- Carefully place pot on a sturdy table. Since too much heat can over-stimulate the skin and break delicate capillaries, the skin's tiny network of blood vessels, it's important to sit no closer than two feet from the steamy mixture. *Do not lean directly over the pot!*
- With eyes closed, allow the gentle mist to "brush" the skin for ten to fifteen minutes.
- Rinse face with tepid, not cold, water. Tepid water will not shock your skin or weaken its elasticity.
- Now you are ready for a superficial "peeling." In an upward, outward motion, gently apply oatmeal scrub to skin, avoiding the delicate eye area. Since pores are open, it's important to be light-handed with the scrub. Let it "mask" the skin five minutes while you rest with feet slightly elevated. *Do not apply this scrub if you have acne or if your skin is irritated.*
- Thoroughly rinse with tepid water.
- Finish with a mild mask. Plain yogurt or mashed avocado, applied for ten to fifteen minutes, tightens pores. Tepid rinse again.
- Lightly apply moisturizing cream. You won't need a heavy coating since penetration is excellent now that pores are open.

SAUNA WITH LOOFAH

This fibrous skeleton of the fruit of a loofah is earth's natural sponge. The loofah stimulates circulation and *epiabrades,* removing dead cells from the surface of the skin.

During the skin's normal renewal process called *exfoliation,* it's these old cells which make skin feel dry and look flaky.

Regular buffing with a loofah is the best way to smooth the surface and it's a wonderful treat for your body. Pay close attention to elbows, knees and heels.

Sauna is effective in eliminating wastes from the body. Wet sauna or turkish baths are best since moisture in the air replenishes skin, leaving it

Photo: George Selman. Makeup: Rudy Calvo

soft. Kim says a wet sauna, plus loofah, is the perfect way to polish your body!

Here are additional tips:
- A wet sauna or steam is better for your skin than a dry sauna.
- Drink plenty of water. Because perspiration causes your body to lose water, drinking beforehand will prevent dehydration.
- Sit in sauna for two six-minute intervals. Once your body begins to perspire after a few minutes, gently scrub your upper body, remembering to always work in the direction toward the heart. *Do not sit in the sauna for more than five or six minutes. Excess heat can cause dizziness and fainting. Also, too much moisture loss can disturb the elasticity and tenacity of the skin.*
- Take a cool shower to close pores.
- Return to sauna for second interval, no longer than six minutes. Gently scrub lower body, again working upward, toward the heart.
- Take a final, cool shower to close pores.

Kim suggests not wearing a thermal suit into the sauna. It keeps heat in the body, preventing the body's proper regulation of temperature. The result is overheating, which can put you into a state of shock.

"Controlled perspiration is an excellent way to release wastes," she summarizes, "but too much perspiration robs the body of needed vitamins and minerals."

Before using *any* sauna, check with your doctor to preclude the presence of health problems. Sauna is *not* recommended for women with heart trouble, anemia, high blood pressure or any blood or circulatory illness.

BEAUTY/SPORT VACATIONS

When we think of a vacation to unwind, thoughts usually fly to remote beaches or exotic retreats across the water. However, right within our shores, from the East Coast to the West, is a sprinkling of spas offering what we pursue most in vacations—rest, mental serenity, physical refreshment . . . and fun!

For the woman in search of the all-embracing, luxurious experience, a spa vacation may be just what the doctor ordered.

In addition to aromatherapy, there are spas offering *thalassotherapy,* skin treatments with mineral-rich seawater and sea plants, and *hydrotherapy,* therapeutic underwater massage.

Some spas give a combination of treatments or tailor a regimen to your

Teenage makeover, *Musanna Overr,* is an example that well-blended colors are best on a young complexion. For her *red undertones,* cool shades like berry reds and reds are perfect makeup colors for lips and cheeks.

Ingram Engram, a secretary, has *yellow undertones.* For cheeks and lips, warm colors like soft russets, terra-cotta, clear reds or peach are perfect for business/daytime makeup. Cool colors—roses, pinks—are great for evening.

Scriptwriter *Jean Johnson* has *orange undertones.* Warm colors that have just a hint of orange tones work best on her cheeks and lips. Deep corals bring out that pretty, subtle blush and are perfect for daytime or evening makeup. Makeup by Rudy Calvo.

Color photos by George Selman.

For sport, *Naima's* makeup is nothing more than a hint of color blended to a whisper on her eyes. Lips are well moisturized for protection while playing outdoors. A French braid and open-ended wisps are easy to do and give hair a carefree twist. Makeup: Rudy Calvo. Hair: Pam Eatmon for John Atchison.

When it's time for college classes, Naima is the perfect student. Hair is set in deep waves for a more polished look. For the freshest makeup, yellow, taupe and brown are blended on eyes. Sheer terra-cotta on lips and cheeks accent yellow undertones. Makeup: LaLette Littlejohn. Hair: Sterfon Demings for John Atchison.

Mrs. Anna Velasquez is a teacher, wife and mother of three with one granchild. This step-by-step makeover transforms her from a beautiful "Mom" into a stunning evening look. Hair/Makeup, LaLette Littlejohn.

1. Before—Mrs. Velasquez has yellow undertones.

2. Cover-up, blended under eyes and on smile line, evens skin tone.

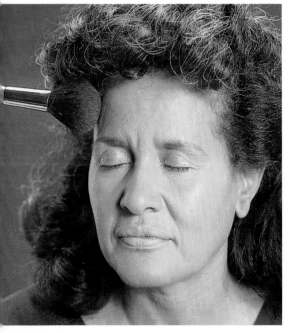

3. A ruddy beige foundation is applied to face and neck. A translucent powder, brushed right into hairline, "sets" makeup.

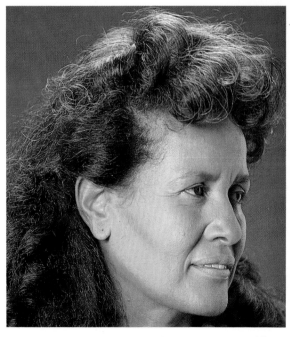

4. Contouring right under cheekbones adds definition to cheeks.

5. Cheeks are blushed with a deep rose color and lips are lined with a soft red liner.

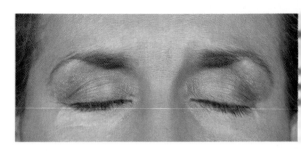

6. A violet shadow accents eyes. To open eyes, a blue pencil brightens eyes. Next, lashes are coated with mascara; brows are brushed up.

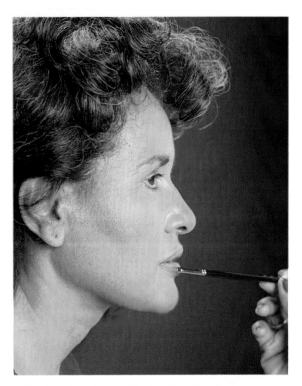

7. A pale color applied to lips first is the perfect primer for a bold cranberry lipstick.

After—Hair is swept up for the perfect evening style. Hair/Makeup, LaLette Littlejohn.

THE COMPLETE MAKEOVER

At twenty-eight years old, *Juanda Green* weighed 188 pounds. A single mother, she holds a master's degree in Biblical Counseling.

By eating nutritiously, she lost forty pounds in eleven months.

THE HAIR STORY

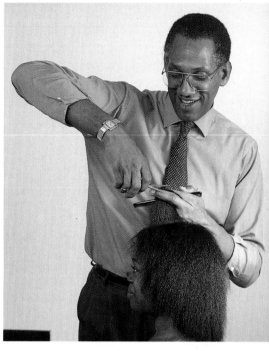

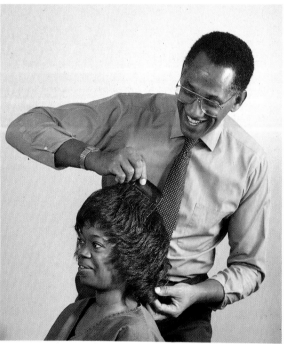

Above left, Juanda has clear skin and a beautiful complexion. Her undertones are yellow. To begin her makeover, a haircut and style are the first steps.

Above right, after a mild relaxer is applied and hair is shampooed and blown dry, John Atchison dry-cuts Juanda's hair to slim and balance her features. Hair is cut longer at the crown to minimize fullness around the cheek and jawline area. Hair is trimmed so that it stays long at the back to balance the cut, and loosely curled using a curling wand. Wispy bangs at the forehead add softness to her full face.

Left, using a special, wide-tooth comb, John styles Juanda's hair. He combs her hair forward so that it gently frames her forehead and cheeks. He emphasizes the style by defining each row with the tip of the comb.

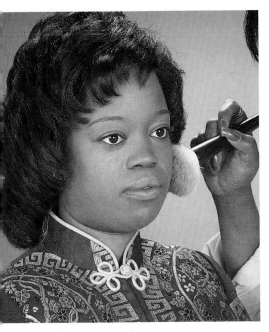 

Left, makeup artist LaLette Littlejohn tweezes stray hairs from Juanda's brow to "open" her eyes. Facial hairs above her lip and around the chin are removed with a depilatory that's especially designed for faces. A toner soothes her skin before foundation is applied. A dusting of loose powder completes the first makeup steps.

Right, contouring cheeks with a brick-colored powder heightens and accentuates Juanda's cheekbones. Next, LaLette shades underneath Juanda's chin to minimize the roundness of her face.

Left, eyes get lots of color! First, LaLette applies a rose color in the crease of the eye and violet at the edges of the lid. To accent eyes, a blue line under the bottom lid is smudged and softened with an applicator. The same blue pencil rims upper lid. False eyelashes complete Juanda's eye appeal.

Right, lips are lined with a pencil slightly darker than lipcolor. A deep rose lipcolor is then applied with a lipbrush and blotted to a matte finish with a tissue.

The makeover is now complete. With a forty-pound weight loss, plus the right hair and makeup, Juanda is transformed from simply beautiful to a *stunning beauty!*

specific needs. Usually, the week is centered on fitness, relaxation, nutritional adaptation and massage. Makeup consultation and cooking lessons may even be included!

To suit the palate of the adventurous, there are also fitness cruises which offer the ultimate, active vacation. And sports-centered weeks at tennis camps feature professional advice for beginners, intermediate and advanced. In addition to perfecting your sport, there's the priceless adventure of meeting others who share your enthusiasm for the game.

Other vacation options are adult camps where people can learn to build boats, climb mountains or survive in the great outdoors away from "civilization."

Granted, such treats are not inexpensive, and though refreshing, beauty/sports vacations do not satisfy the quest of exploring your roots. But, should you plan not to venture abroad, these are just a few exciting alternatives you may enjoy at home. Your travel agent can offer more suggestions.

You've worked diligently all year to deserve that week away. Why not choose a vacation that works just as hard for you?

COSMETIC CHALLENGES

Our appearance affects how we feel about ourselves. For women who suffer with acne and the skin disorder vitiligo, there's good news! Successful treatments by leading dermatologists offer hope and can result in a new you.

ACNE'S ROOTS

According to Dr. James William Hobbs, M.D., associate professor of dermatology at King-Drew Medical Center in Los Angeles, "The beginnings of acne lie deep in the root where hair grows."

Although concentrated on the scalp, hair is present all over the body, except on the palm of the hand and sole of the foot. It's the overproduction of sebum, or oil, in the fine, facial hairs which results in *acne.*

Once too much sebum is produced, it clumps together with cells. What results is a blackhead or a whitehead.

A blackhead in clinical terms is called an *open comedo.* The surface is open and black, due to the buildup of pigment cells, oil and bacteria. A whitehead is called a *closed comedo* because the surface is closed and white.

Dr. Hobbs points out that everyone has normal bacterial flora, but in acne, one of these bacteria builds up and causes an inflammatory reaction.

"The body responds to this as a foreign material and creates pus in a foreign-body reaction. Clinically, we see this as papules and pustules."

While *papules* are just slight, reddish elevations signaling an early inflammatory reaction, *pustules* are more extensive, aggressive reactions. *Cysts* and *nodules* are acne's most severe inflammations.

With any inflammatory reaction comes the disruption of *melanocytes,* pigment cells. This causes the most distress among Black women, because of the unsightly, persistent *postinflammatory hyperpigmentation,* dark marks, which result from acne's irritation. Harsh scrubbing or picking the skin can also cause dark marks.

"The more severe the inflammation, the more the chance of hyperpigmentation," says Dr. Hobbs. Interestingly enough, of all of his patients, nearly half come in primarily for treatment to get rid of the dark marks.

"Unfortunately, they do not come in for treatment earlier, during acne's inflammatory period. I stress to these patients that acne is what causes these unsightly dark marks. Therefore, it's important to treat the acne."

To treat hyperpigmentation, a cream containing a higher amount of the skin bleach *hydroquinone* is often prescribed. (See the chapter "Lovely Complexions" for more discussion.) The dermatologist's prescription can contain more hydroquinone than that in over-the-counter products.

ACNE TREATMENT

Dermatologist Greta Clarke, M.D., who is in private practice in Berkeley, California, stresses that treatment for acne varies from patient to patient.

"Skin type, such as oily or dry, is a primary factor in determining the best treatment. Also, a combination of medications may be prescribed if there are papules or pustules."

Benzoyl peroxide, an over-the-counter topical application which destroys bacteria, is still an effective treatment. *Acutane,* a prescribed medication, may be indicated for more severe, cystic acne.

Collagen injections are only temporary, but help fill in depressed, ice-pick scars that result from severe acne. *Hypertrophic scars,* scars which are slightly elevated, can be flattened by injections of steroids. *Keloids,* shiny scars which are noticeably raised above the surface of the skin, require the attention of a skilled cosmetic surgeon. A discussion of keloids is in the following chapter.

Dermabrasion, or sanding of the skin so that the complexion is once again smooth, is another way to erase skin depressions caused by acne. Since melanin is important in the healing process, some discoloration may occur, but its effect may only be temporary. Dermabrading the entire face and "feathering" the skin around the eye area minimizes the problem of abrupt margins. Your dermatologist can best advise you. Deep, ice-pick scars may require two treatments—primary scar revision followed by dermabrasion in six to eight weeks.

ADULT ACNE

While it is expected that teenagers will experience acne flare-ups, adults who get acne in their mid- to late twenties are usually caught off guard.

"Stress is often a factor in adult acne," Dr. Clarke explains. "Also, hormonal imbalances play a part, as does a sensitivity to iodine in the diet, or reactions to chocolate and cola."

For these individuals, shellfish should be avoided, and mineral supplements and vitamin preparations containing iodine should be eliminated.

COMEDOGENIC

Because cosmetics can contribute to acne's untimely appearance, *comedogenic* is a term which became popular in the mid-1980's. Dr. Clarke explains what comedogenic actually means.

"In studies examining the effect of moisturizers and makeup on skin, oils were rubbed onto rabbits' ears to see their effect. It was found that these oils produced comedones—whiteheads and blackheads. Many cosmetic companies are sensitive to this now and have made the transition to noncomedogenic moisturizers."

Petrolatum and baby oil are highly comedogenic and are certainly to be avoided for anyone with a tendency toward acne.

"Women who may not have reacted to petrolatum and baby oil before may find that they start to develop whiteheads and blackheads over a period of time. Overall, it's better for everyone to use preparations that are less oily," suggests Dr. Clarke.

Similarly, cocoa butter is a comedogenic agent. "Sometimes women with acne who develop hyperpigmentation will use cocoa butter, believing the myth that cocoa butter will lighten dark spots. But what it actually does is worsen the acne, because cocoa butter is comedogenic. Also, it contains no hydroquinone and it is therefore totally ineffective in treating dark marks."

No matter how tempting, wearing makeup is highly discouraged during acne's flare-up. Skin which is already experiencing a breakout can be further irritated, prolonging the healing process.

VITILIGO

Vitiligo is a cosmetic disorder in which *hypopigmentation,* loss of pigment, causes areas of white patches to appear on the skin.

"Most people believe vitiligo is more common among Blacks or darker-complected individuals. But this is not so," explains Pearl E. Grimes, M.D., assistant professor of dermatology at King-Drew Medical Center and UCLA School of Medicine in Los Angeles.

"There is no difference in incidence among ethnic groups. In dark complexions, however, loss of pigment—sharp contrasts of black and white skin —is obviously more apparent."

While vitiligo can appear in random patches all over the body, it can also be confined to one particular area, such as on the face and extremities, or appear along a particular nerve distribution. Genetics has a hand in this skin disorder. Vitiligo runs in families.

What causes vitiligo? "Many dermatologists suspect an autoimmune theory: the body becomes allergic to its own melanocytes or pigment cells, and sends antibodies or other substances to attack and destroy them."

Vitiligo is associated with other autoimmune conditions. "Patients with vitiligo may have a predisposition to an overactive or underactive thyroid, diabetes mellitus, rheumatoid arthritis, pernicious anemia or atopic dermatitis. Once vitiligo is diagnosed, the individual should be thoroughly examined to preclude the presence of these disorders as well."

Premature graying and *alopecia areata,* patchy hair loss, are common among vitiligo patients and their families.

The psychological effects of vitiligo, mirrored in those who have sharp contrasts of pigmentation, can be devastating. Many suffer from extreme depression and low self-esteem.

"The emphasis society places on physical appearance can cause tremendous anxiety in people with vitiligo. Even if they make attempts to accept their condition, society often does not."

TREATMENT

Treatment for vitiligo is successful in many patients thanks to *psoralin,* a drug which stimulates melanocytes to repigment the skin. The results are dramatic.

Psoralin is applied topically, or "painted" onto the hypopigmented area. After an interval of thirty minutes to an hour, the area is exposed to ultraviolet light.

In cases where vitiligo is extensive, covering most of the body, *depigmenting,* or removing pigment from normal cells so that there is a uniformity of white complexion, is another option. *Monobenzyl ether of hydroquinone,* the most potent bleaching cream on the market, irreversibly destroys pigment cells.

"Not everyone is a candidate for depigmentation. The overall psychological impact on the patient and the family deserves careful consideration," cautions Dr. Grimes.

In less severe cases, vitiligo can also be masked cosmetically. For effective coverage, Dr. Grimes recommends Dermablend by Flori Roberts.

First, experts blend shades to exactly match the natural color of skin. Next, the opaque, concealing makeup is applied directly onto the white patches, or blended all over the face, so that skin now has one uniform color.

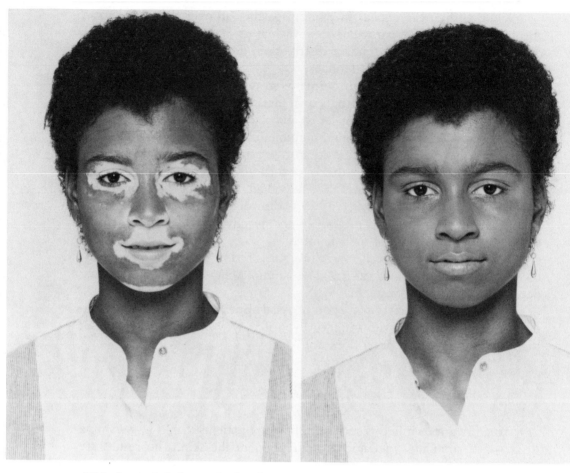

This dramatic before-and-after demonstrates how effectively vitiligo can be cosmetically masked with concealing makeup.

Dusting a special loose powder which seals the foundation so that it becomes waterproof is the final step. Makeup is easily removed with a liquid cleanser.

BROWN MOLES

Dermatitis papulosa nigra, also called DPNs, are tiny black or brown moles which appear on the face, neck, chest or upper back in as many as eight out of ten Black adults. Although perfectly harmless and painless, they can be bothersome, especially if they are plentiful on the face.

DPNs can be surgically "lifted" off the skin with *cryotherapy* or *light desiccation* by a dermatologist. Scraping is not advised, since it can cause discoloration.

FOR MORE INFORMATION

Outlined above are just a few of the cosmetic challenges which black women may face. If you would like more information, write the National Medical Association, 1012 Tenth Street, NW, Washington, DC 20001.

AESTHETIC APPEAL

Black women are opting for cosmetic surgery in increasing numbers. Noses are refined, lips are brought into facial harmony, wrinkles tucked, lines erased and tummies, breasts and buttocks reduced.

While these procedures are certainly not new, what is novel is that more and more of us are free to choose elective surgery. Is the zeal for aesthetic appeal for the right reason, or is it an attempt to deny our ethnic heritage?

WHY COSMETIC SURGERY?

Harold E. Pierce, M.D., assistant professor of dermatology and soft-tissue surgery, Howard University College of Medicine, and in private practice in Bala Cynwyd, Pennsylvania, has been a pioneer in dermatologic and cosmetic surgery for black skins. He offers this skilled observation in addressing the question of cosmetic surgery and ethnic heritage.

"While it is true that a few people attempt to conceal their ethnic origins through cosmetic surgery," says Dr. Pierce, "the majority of people choose surgery purely to improve their self-image."

Stressing that there are times when a woman has a legitimate concern over the size of her nose or the lack of a defined chin, Dr. Pierce points out that more and more people are having these procedures in growing numbers. According to the American Society of Plastic and Reconstructive Surgeons, over 590,000 Americans had cosmetic surgery last year.

"Other ethnic groups vying for social acceptance among their peers have no problem undergoing rhinoplasty—nose jobs—or chin implantation. These surgical adventures are pursued in the interest of improving self-image by enhancing facial artistic harmony."

More and more Black Americans are entering economic categories which afford them the luxury of change. The climb up the ladder of success carries with it financial rewards and the option to gain added acceptance, especially in careers where the spotlight is on appearance.

Photo: Bobby Isais

"We learn the importance of appearance very early. Pretty children are teachers' pets. Later, we see that attractive employment applicants have the edge in the job market. Whether this means that the less attractive are constantly rejected by society or become antisocial is still under investigation by sociologists."

Dr. Pierce explains that in the facial analysis, the objective of cosmetic surgery is total harmony. "In nature, symmetry is the rule rather than the exception." Nose, lips, chin should complement each other. Achieving this surgically is not a denial of heritage.

"The goal of cosmetic surgery is to decaricaturize awkward-appearing features which contribute grossly to an unbalanced physical image," explains Dr. Pierce.

"Just as there are facial profiles of white patients that are disharmonious, so, too, does disharmony occur among Black patients. The woman who chooses to improve her facial appearance is not attempting to have Caucasian features imposed on her nonwhite face."

SURVEY

A survey of three thousand cosmetic patients revealed that most did not hope to alter their ethnic heritage or even become "beautiful." Rather, they wanted to downplay what they considered to be a prominent defect in their appearance and modify that feature which caused others to "look back" or take a second look.

The survey also demonstrates that when cosmetic surgery is performed for good reasons, the results are so gratifying that the quality of the patient's life is actually enhanced.

"The woman who exhibits a magnitude of pride in grooming and who has confidence in her personal appearance is most likely to consider cosmetic surgery," says Dr. Pierce.

CONSULTATION AND EVALUATION

Because physicians are aware that some emotionally unhealthy candidates do present themselves for surgical procedures, careful consultation and evaluation usually precede any operation. To many surgeons, this is the most critical step.

According to Napoleon Vaughn, Ph.D., a psychologist in private practice in Philadelphia who works closely with Dr. Pierce and who is also on staff at Northwest Psychiatric Institute in Fort Washington, Pennsylvania, these four principles should be included in every evaluation:

1. Does the patient have a legitimate reason for wanting the surgical procedure? Is there an obvious cosmetic disfigurement? Does the deformity appear grossly disfiguring to other people, or only to the patient?
2. Does the patient have a high level of ego strength? Or, once stripped of this deformity, will the prospective patient feel naked and vulnerable?
3. Has the patient clearly heard, and correctly restated in totality, the explanation of what is realistic to expect? Or does the patient hope to become "beautiful" overnight and have her entire life change because of the operation?
4. Does the patient exhibit an emotional balance and basic security by clear, verbal expression? Or, does she hint at emotional impairment by an inability to talk? Is she nonresponsive, dull or withdrawn? Is there poor eye contact?

The absolute *wrong* reason is to please someone else, like husband or boyfriend because he feels nose/lips/chin are imperfect.

And, warns Dr. Vaughn, "there's a keg of danger in believing that cosmetic surgery will automatically solve all the problems in the world. Improvement, rather than change, is the correct focus."

More and more Black women are becoming aware of their self-image and are taking healthy steps to improve, through cosmetic surgery, their physical attributes. Wanting to look better so that you can feel better about yourself is the *right* reason.

COSMETIC PROCEDURES

Following is a description of cosmetic procedures which can be performed by a qualified cosmetic surgeon. The best way to choose a surgeon is by personal referral. People who are satisfied with their doctors are the best advertisement. The American Society of Plastic and Reconstructive Surgeons in Chicago, can also provide you with a list of board-certified surgeons in your area.

Rhytidoplasty—A face-lift, surgically tightens the skin so that it is once again smooth with a firm, younger appearance. A full face-lift involves removal of excess tissue from the cheek, neck and temporal areas. In a modified face-lift, only the skin at the cheek and neck is tightened. It takes several weeks for the swelling to completely subside.

Another procedure is an operation which flattens the nasolabial fold around the mouth to reduce sagging cheeks. Before you consider a more extensive face-lift, ask your cosmetic surgeon about this procedure. It may be all the "lift" your face really needs.

Chemical Peel—Fine lines and wrinkles can be removed by chemical peel, also called *chemosurgery.* A chemical, *phenol,* peels away the top layer of skin to reveal fresh, new skin. Since the complexion is 10 to 20 percent lighter postpeel, chemosurgery is best performed on women who have fairer complexions.

Blepharoplasty—Baggy, puffy eyes, sometimes caused by heredity, can make you look as if you're feeling "sad." Surgery of the eyelids is an effective way to correct droopy, puffy eyes or to remove bags from underneath the eyes.

Otoplasty—Combing your hair over your ears to hide protruding ears is certainly one solution. More permanent, however—and more liberating—is to have ears surgically corrected. Otoplasty also restructures deformed or flattened ears and is a popular procedure for children as well as adults.

Rhinoplasty—Resculpting the nose by removing excess bone or cartilage and molding the skin over the new surface is probably one of the most popular forms of cosmetic surgery among all ethnic groups. With more discretionary income, Black women—and men—are equally enjoying the benefits of this surgical option.

The goal should not be to create a "new" nose but to bring the existing nose into harmony with eyes, lips and overall facial structures. Sometimes the best restructured nose is the one that's hardly noticed!

Because removal of bone is involved, there is some discomfort, swelling and discoloration after the operation.

If you wear eyeglasses, you may have the added expense of changing them to fit your new nose. Or you may even decide to toss them completely and wear contact lenses instead. With newer lenses that can also alter your eye color, this can be a pretty proposition.

Whatever your decision, remember that rhinoplasty can change the way you look. It cannot change your life. But once you feel better about the way you look, perhaps *you* can change your life.

Cheiloplasty—Cheiloplasty, or lip reduction, corrects the hereditary condition of oversized lips. After surgery, excessive talking and chewing are discouraged for seven to ten days.

Mammaplasty—Surgical procedures to enlarge or reduce breasts are termed mammaplasty. Implants to augment breasts help bolster a positive self-image for the woman who is extremely self-conscious about having small breasts. Reduction mammaplasty takes the weight off women whose shoulders and back are burdened by the strain of pendulous bosoms.

Both procedures are expensive, but the benefits far outweigh the financial investment. "Acceptable" scars which result from these cosmetic surgical procedures may be easily concealed by wearing a normal bra or bathing suit.

Apart from cosmetic surgery, little can be done to improve the size of breasts, but proper bra support—especially during exercise—is essential in maintaining an uplifting shape.

Body-Contouring—Fat deposits result in bulging skin on arms, abdomen, hips, thighs and buttocks. They can be surgically removed through *liposuction,* a high-pressure vacuum suction which extracts fat cells through tiny incisions in the skin.

Although incorrectly thought to be a quick fix for women who are overweight, there is a limit to the amount of fat which can be safely removed. Women who are already on an exercise program and who eat a moderate diet are the best candidates.

Over forty is the recommended age for most body-contouring or sculpting. Since women have an extra layer of fat below the navel for childbearing, a tummy tuck, or *abdominoplasty,* is best performed following the reproductive years. The recommended recovery time is six to eight weeks.

PAID IN ADVANCE

With cosmetic surgery, there are no guarantees. Surgeons usually require that the total cost of the procedure be paid in full prior to surgery. In most instances, insurance will not cover the expense of elective surgery.

Expect a consultation fee for preoperative evaluation. And, following the surgery, money will *not* be refunded should there be any discontentment with the results.

The cosmetic surgeon may also provide other services, such as makeup consultation. His objective? To assist the patient in accenting her new features.

THE KELOID QUESTION

With the discussion of cosmetic surgery for Black women comes the *keloid* question. A keloid is a large, shiny mass which results from a scar that "forgets" to stop growing.

For decades, the special concerns of Black women went neglected because of the fear of keloid formation and scarring. Similarly, dermabrasion for darker-skinned people was not recommended.

Dr. Pierce, who performed his first dermabrasion nearly thirty years ago, believes that Black women can experience the same benefits of surgery as do women of other ethnic groups.

"It's a myth to say that all black skins form keloids in the healing process," he stresses. "Through careful examination of medical history, the surgeon can determine whether or not keloidal formation is part of the patient's normal pattern of healing. Even if keloids are a problem, precautions can be taken to prevent this pile-up of unsightly scar tissue."

Scar revision, the removal of keloids, is another area pioneered by Dr. Pierce. After the keloid has been surgically lifted, a pressure bandage forces the scar to reheal without extending beyond the normal boundary of the skin's surface. Injections of cortisone and X-ray therapy enhance the beneficial effects.

A. Paul Kelly, M.D., head of dermatology at King-Drew Medical Center in Los Angeles, also specializes in treatment and removal of keloids. He reports that early treatment with X-ray therapy prevents young keloids from forming.

In determining who is most likely to form keloids Dr. Kelly makes this observation: "Just because a woman forms keloids behind her earlobes does not mean she will form keloids elsewhere. It may be an indication, but it's not 100 percent predictable."

To remove a keloid from behind the ears, Dr. Kelly first excises it. Then at intervals of two to three weeks, he gives intralesional—into the postoperative site—injections of steroids. During healing time, a special pressure earring is worn for several months.

"Normal healing occurs within forty-two days, but since keloids result from an abnormal healing process, the pressure earring is worn much longer to prevent any pile-up of scar tissue."

COSMETIC DENTISTRY

Perhaps nothing uplifts a face and brightens the eyes more than an attractive smile. Correcting chipped teeth, closing front gaps and covering yellow tobacco stains are as effective in improving appearance as a face-lift.

According to Jerry Albus, D.D.S., in Burbank, California, front teeth deserve special attention. "Cosmetic dentistry corrects any defect that makes a person feel self-conscious or look unattractive."

Crowns, an artificial covering made of acrylic, metal and porcelain, are a beautiful and permanent solution to replace uneven or damaged teeth.

Direct bonding, a technique perfected by Dr. Albus's colleague Don Kobashigawa, D.D.S., is perhaps one of the most revolutionary techniques. This painless process can be completed quickly and lasts from four to eight years. Tooth-colored plastic, painted onto the front surface of stained or damaged teeth, resurfaces the area and is effective in closing gaps. Best of all, there's no drilling.

Beautiful teeth make any woman feel more confident. No matter how long you may have waited, it's never too late to perfect that smile.

Making Up

MAKEUP IN MINUTES

Now you're ready for makeup! And with the right tools and know-how, a few minutes—from foundation to mascara—are all it takes for a basic, every-day look.

In this section, I'll share my expertise gleaned from my years as a beauty and health editor.

A checklist of basic tools and cosmetics helps you organize your makeup wardrobe. "Tools of the Trade" spells out exactly what you'll need for home, purse, travel and sport, so that you're always prepared.

Next, a simple approach to "Finding the Perfect Color" takes the guess-work out of choosing makeup. Knowing your undertone helps you find the right colors to accent your good looks.

In "Four Makeup Looks," you'll see how easy it is to apply your makeup for sport, daytime/business, evening and formal. To illustrate the transfor-mation that occurs with the right makeup, before-and-after photographs ap-pear in the eight-page color section.

A spritz of fragrance, manicure and pedicure complete your beauty pic-ture. How to body-layer for a sensual you is one of the perks discussed in "Finishing Touches."

This makeup section is designed not to add to, but to highlight the beauty that's already inside. And it demonstrates what we've known all these years: when a Black woman is beautiful, she's like nothing else the world has ever seen!

TOOLS OF THE TRADE

You don't have to spend a fortune to look like a million. A few inexpensive tools of the trade will give you as professional a look as if you had spent a bundle. And since it's a good idea to replace your items periodically, the wise choice is to save money where you can so you can splurge when you want.

Also discussed in this chapter: how to organize your cosmetics and toiletries for purse, home, travel and sport.

Brushes and cosmetics, courtesy Avon. Photo: George Selman

JUST IN CASE

Two makeup cases, a medium-size one to store easily at home and a smaller one for your purse, will help keep cosmetics right at your fingertips. And when you need to travel for business or pleasure, packing is easy. Just grab your bag, because everything you will need is already in the case.

In the home cosmetic case pack these basics, starting with the tools you will need.

Keep:
- The fattest brush for powder
- A medium brush for blush
- Lip brush to apply sheer color
- Makeup sponge for blending
- Shadow brush for eyecolor
- Tweezers to remove stray eyebrow hairs
- Brow comb for lashes and brows
- Smudger to blend eye makeup
- Tissues for blending, cleaning

And the cosmetics you will need:
- Cover stick
- Sheer water-based foundation
- Translucent powder
- Blush compact
- A dark shadow for contouring
- Eye shadow compact with at least three colors
- Eyeliner/eyebrow pencil
- Mascara
- Lip liner pencil
- Lipstick

IN THE PURSE

For the case in your purse, keeping the absolute minimal means you always travel light and right.

Pack:
- Blush compact

- Lip liner
- Lip moisturizer
- Lipstick
- Powder compact
- Tissues

And, so you'll never be caught unprepared, add a travel toothbrush, a string of floss, tiny tube of toothpaste, a small wide-tooth comb and a travel-size of your favorite perfume for a refreshing spritz anytime, anywhere.

SOFT TOUCHES

For a soft touch in makeup application, cotton, cotton swabs, tissues and cosmetic squares are like best friends for your face.

Cotton moistened in makeup remover gently cleanses your face; cotton swabs help smudge edges; tissues clean up during makeup application and are great to blot excess oil during the day; cosmetic squares are useful in removing makeup and applying toner at night.

And have you ever applied your makeup so that it is absolutely perfect, only to realize you must now slip your silk dress or white sweater *over* your head? Here is where a long scarf folded in your makeup drawer comes in handy.

Drape it loosely around hair and face before quickly slipping on clothes. Both hair and makeup will remain intact. You will also appreciate not getting traces of makeup on your clean garments.

STASHING EXTRA MAKEUP

Storage of extra makeup is easy with a plastic fishing-tackle box. The layers of drawers and sectioned spaces allow you to conveniently stash those colors you don't use everyday.

Keep nail polishes, remover and tools for toes and nails in a small, separate case altogether. Choose one with a lining that will not be ruined if there is an accidental spill.

TRAVEL POUCH

A toiletry/cosmetics travel pouch is a "must have" if you're a woman who travels frequently. No matter how little time there is for you to get prepared for that plane, packing will be a cinch with this pouch at the ready.

A large lined pouch is what you'll need. Choose one with a fabric covering so you can wash it outside, as well as inside, periodically. Pockets and zippered compartments make organizing even more efficient.

Since, for me, there's nothing worse than getting off a plane only to find out that my luggage is taking some exotic excursion, my travel pouch stays with me at all times. I pack it, along with my cosmetics case, a good book and running shoes, right in my carry-on bag.

There's a little bit of everything in the travel pouch. I add cosmetics, toiletries and miscellaneous items gradually, sometimes purchasing two of whatever I'm buying so the extra can be tucked away just for travel. Keeping this pouch stocked at all times eliminates the worry that I'll forget my moisturizer!

And have you ever wondered what on earth to do with all those sample treatment products, cosmetics and trial-size perfumes? Stock them in your travel pouch and have fun experimenting in your hotel room.

Smallest, travel-size plastic bottles and containers—the *tiniest*—minimize bulk. Posttravel, replenish whatever's depleted.

Here's my checklist:
- Moisturizer
- Facial soap or cleanser
- Cleansing grains
- Facial mask
- Toning lotion
- Under eye cream
- Shower soap
- Toothbrush/floss
- Toothpaste
- Mouthwash
- Shampoo
- Conditioner/cream rinse
- Disposable razor
- Bobby pins/hairpins
- Cotton balls
- Shower cap
- Hair spray
- Antiperspirant
- Talc
- Tampons/sanitary napkins

- Aspirin
- Sewing kit
- Emery board
- Nail polish/remover
- Small loofah
- Perfumed body lotion
- Perfume

AND . . . SPORT BAG

While I'm on a roll, let me throw in one more prepacked bag. It makes going to the gym or spa hassle-free.

Toss in:

- Massage oil
- Shampoo
- Loofah
- Body lotion
- Soap
- Antiperspirant
- Tampons/sanitary napkins
- Toothbrush/toothpaste
- Moisturizer
- Hairpins/coated rubber bands

FINDING THE PERFECT COLOR

With over thirty skin tones for Black women, finding the perfect color for foundation, lips and cheeks can be a frustrating task. No more! My simple solution explained in these pages is specifically designed to take the guesswork out of color selection. It proves that, after all, making up is *really* not hard to do.

LESS IS MORE

Like the old-fashioned rule that cautions against adding just one accessory too much, when it comes to makeup, less is definitely more.

Sometimes even the smallest amount of makeup looks obvious because the colors are all wrong. Rather than blending in with the skin tone, the makeup stands out in definite contrast with skin coloring. No matter how smartly makeup is applied, it ends up looking like "too much."

There is a way to avoid this mistake and choose the perfect color for your complexion. Here is my formula specially designed to help take the guesswork out of choosing makeup colors.

BROWN . . . PLUS

When you look at your skin, what do you see? In addition to brown, do you see a little red . . . a hint of yellow . . . or a bit of orange?

That color you see in addition to your brown color is what I call your *undertone.* And your undertone is the additional color to consider with any makeup you apply to face, eyes, cheeks, lips.

Your undertone is your key in selecting foundation base and makeup colors that blend so perfectly with your skin tone you'll hardly know you're wearing any makeup at all. That means you can enhance your best features or "cover" your imperfections without looking overly made up.

THE RIGHT FOUNDATION

For us, our biggest makeup challenge is finding the right foundation color. When out of luck, mixing shades to blend the perfect color has been the next best solution.

But frustration mounts when, even with the mixing, the shade still does not exactly match the complexion. That's because there's more to consider than just blending light and dark colors. To get the right foundation shade, you must consider *undertones.*

Look for a foundation color—or colors—with your undertone, whether it's red, yellow or orange. How can you identify your undertone?

If you see a bit of yellow when you look at your face, the back of your hand or inside your wrist, your undertone is yellow. Look for a bit of yellow in the brown foundation you are purchasing. Even if it's a touch lighter or darker than your natural coloring, it will blend better than if the foundation is gray. To warm the skin, a foundation color with just a hint of red is the perfect solution for a sallow complexion.

The same guideline applies for women who have undertones of red and orange. You don't have to study too hard to find your undertone. Just react to what you see. Is there a reddish cast or an orange one?

With the right foundation color, all you have to do is apply a tiny amount for the sheerest finish. Some women avoid wearing makeup altogether because they're afraid to make the wrong decision. But choosing a foundation base according to your undertone means your chances of error are minimized.

And, with the right foundation, one that's not too thick or oily, you'll never look like you have on a mask! Even women with dry skin don't need an oily foundation. A good moisturizer applied *before* the foundation is what dry, flaky skin needs most.

A light-textured, water-base foundation is your most important purchase. Properly applied, your foundation covers flaws and imperfections to give your complexion an even color.

Use fingertips to smooth a liquid base. Carefully blend beneath chin, around edges of jawline into hairline and, if you're wearing hair pulled back or off your face, *in* and around ears.

If your complexion is relatively trouble-free, you do not have to apply foundation all over your face. Just dab on areas you want to even—under eyes, around corners of mouth, above lipline, on any dark spots.

Photo: George Selman. Makeup: Rudy Calvo. Hair: John Atchison

FINISHING POWDER

A translucent finishing powder lightly dusted on forehead, nose, cheeks and chin reduces shine and gives a matte finish that helps makeup last. A bonus, of course, is finding the powder also in your undertone!

Sprinkle a bit of loose powder in palm, dip the tip of a fat brush into powder and sweep over face. Dust until powder is completely blended. Don't forget to dab ears and earlobes.

Allow the powder ten minutes to "warm" with your complexion before deciding it looks too powdery. By the time you're finished applying the rest of your makeup, the powder will have "set."

LIPS AND CHEEKS

Coordinating the perfect lip and cheek colors is especially easy when you know your undertone. The shades suggested below are in "color families" and are grouped according to red, yellow and orange undertones.

The specific shade of the color you select, whether deep and rich or pale and light, depends upon the depth of brown in your natural skin coloring.

When applying cheek color, remember to place the blusher right on the cheekbone and blend into the hairline. There should be no sharp edges or line of demarcation.

Lips are first outlined with a slightly deeper lip liner, then lip color is filled in with a brush and blotted. After applying lip color, don't press lips together. This smears lipstick and ruins the lip liner's definition. Instead, press a tissue between lips to blot excess color.

RED UNDERTONES

Women with red undertones have deep, rich coloring and vibrant complexions. Pale reds, magenta, and reddest reds are bright colors which are the most flattering for cheeks and lips. Wear them boldly!

YELLOW UNDERTONES

What colors are the best accent for medium-toned complexions with golden yellow undertones? Pinks, soft russets, terra-cotta, rose and peach on cheeks and lips give excellent highlights. The majority of black women fall into this category.

ORANGE UNDERTONES

Colors that have just a hint of orange work best on cheeks and lips for women with orange undertones. Auburn hair and freckle-kissed cheeks often distinguish this complexion. Corals, soft browns and pink tones bring out that pretty, subtle blush.

EYECOLORS

When it comes to eye makeup, the color of your pupil—or contact lens!—is your first consideration. Next, the color of clothing, time of day or year and the occasion all dictate eyeshadow color and how subtle or dramatic application need be.

In general, use your favorite fashion colors as guideposts in selecting makeup colors. Those shades which elicit the most compliments would probably do well, softly blended to a wisp on your eyes.

Remember, busy lifestyles mean makeup is simplified. Heavy eye makeup, especially for day, is impractical and unfashionable. Softly defined eyes are more flattering than lots of dark color.

Lining the outer edges of lid with an eye pencil, above top lashes and below bottom lashes, opens up the eye. But lining *inside* the bottom rim of the eye accents under-eye circles and makes eyes appear smaller. If you must line inside, use a blue pencil. It's not as heavy as black, and it makes the whites of the eyes appear whiter.

Nothing accents eyes more than mascara. Most Black women find their lashes don't need curling. Just roll the mascara wand above, then under lashes and lightly brush the tips. *Never* share your mascara wand. That's the easiest way to transfer eye infections.

Brown, rather than black, eye pencil is a more natural color for filling in eyebrows which frame and define eyes. To thicken sparse areas, use tiny, feathered strokes rather than drawing one dark, heavy line.

Leaving brows as natural as possible focuses attention right where you want it. With a tweezer, pluck only stray hairs between brows and under the outer edges. Try to avoid plucking any more than an occasional stray hair above brow.

BEFORE-AND-AFTER MAKEOVERS

To illustrate how transforming it is to select foundation base and makeup colors according to your *undertone,* see the first three makeovers in the color section. They are the best illustrations of how to work with your undertone when you apply your makeup.

Musanna Overr has *red* undertones. Ingra Engram has *yellow* undertones and Jean Johnson has *orange* undertones.

In the next chapter you'll find specific makeup suggestions for sport, daytime/business, evening and formal.

FOUR MAKEUP LOOKS

As women balance lifestyle choices, there is more and more demand for simplicity, efficiency and individuality. We want what works for us—natural, finished makeup that's as special as a fingerprint. In this chapter, four makeup looks are suggested to take you from sport to daytime or business and from evening to formal.

TO WEAR OR NOT . . .

Women who genuinely feel good about who they are don't want to hide behind layers and layers of makeup. The decision to wear makeup or not to wear makeup is purely individual. Some women do opt for the latter. Such purists feel uncomfortable with little more than mascara.

Every woman should have the option of going barefaced! It feels good to be able to get dressed, and with a minimal touch here and there, be done with makeup.

But that means *outside* the complexion must be close to flawless, coupled *inside* with good eating habits and a healthy dose of self-confidence. When that's the case, exercise, sensible eating habits and good skin care give a natural radiance that at times seems a shame to hide.

But there are times when just a little makeup makes a big difference and there are other times when making up to include every detail is what the occasion demands.

SPORT

When it comes to playing indoors or outdoors, healthy, well-cared-for skin deserves showing off. For sport or exercise, what could be more flattering than a freshly cleansed, moisturized face?

When playing outside, look for a moisturizer containing sunscreen. Black skin tans easily, and beautifully. To guard against sun damage from ultraviolet rays that penetrate the skin, a sunscreen is a must.

If you want to avoid tanning, wear a visor or a wide-brimmed hat and select a sunblock or sunscreen with a high sun-protection factor, an SPF of 15. Remember that when you are boating, the sun reflects off the water and you can burn easily if you're not well covered.

To tan, select a sunscreen with a lower sun-protection factor. Look for an SPF of anywhere from 2, for skin that rarely burns, to 8, for skin that always burns and rarely tans.

Remember, cocoa butter and baby oil do not contain any sunscreen and offer no protection against the rays that cause premature aging and skin cancer. Don't forget to rub sunscreen on tops of ears, hands and feet and your husband's bald spot.

To keep lips from feeling or looking dry, a lip balm, also with sunscreen, offers the best protection.

If you must wear makeup, monochromatic color—the same soft tones on lips and cheeks—is just enough to play in.

DAYTIME/BUSINESS

Makeup that's not overdone or too obvious is most appropriate for daytime or business. The look should be clean, tasteful—just enough makeup to accent your best features without looking too made up. What should be noticed in the home, classroom or office is *you,* not your makeup.

Start with an under-eye cover stick. Since skin is thinnest here, blood vessels are more apparent and cause dark circles under the eyes. An undercover stick two shades lighter than foundation minimizes circles. Don't pull skin. Dab inward, always working toward the nose.

Next, apply foundation and blend. Also put foundation on lips to balance color, or use a lip balancer—a flesh-toned lipstick—to give an even tone.

Just the tiniest amount of loose powder is all you'll need for daytime to set foundation and discourage shine.

When it comes to eyes, frosted, pearlized colors, even when in style, may still be better for evening than daytime. What's fashionable for the quickest daytime eyes? Sweep one neutral color on lid, crease and brow.

Mascara is a must. A thin coating on top and bottom lashes gives a finished look to your makeup.

Photo: George Selman. Makeup: Rudy Calvo. Hair: John Atchison

For subtle color on lips, line them in the same color as lipstick before applying color with a lip brush for thin, even coverage.

EVENING

Applying makeup from day to evening follows the same principle as layering a shawl over a jacket. Add just a little more color so that the effect is deeper, more intense.

For evening, shading and contouring crease of eyes, sides of nose and just underneath cheekbone gives definition to your face that's so attractive in soft, romantic lighting. A new dusting of powder, on neck too, and a little more polish on cheeks is just right for night.

Eyecolors can offer a bit more drama. Rimming eyes with a smoky shade makes eyes look larger. Smudge color just underneath bottom lashes and just above upper lashes, but don't line *inside*. Use a thin shadow brush and powder eyeshadow rather than a pencil for the softest line. And do add more mascara.

To heighten lip color, use a liner slightly darker than you do for daytime. Then add a richer-colored lipstick, again applied with a brush for even coverage.

FORMAL

You'll want to go all out in applying your formal makeup. Extravagant, luxurious, glamorous and sophisticated are words which describe the look you want to achieve for that special occasion.

Apply under-eye coverstick. For a matte foundation that lasts and lasts, you may want to use a pancake makeup which gives more complete coverage. Apply only a sheer layer with a damp makeup sponge and blend, blend, blend.

With the fattest brush, dust face with translucent powder. Now, contour to shape and define cheeks, nose, eyes. Some colors used for contouring can make your face look "dirty," so be careful to choose a color—plum rather than brown—that's not too dark. Apply color just underneath cheekbones and along sides of nose to make the area recede.

After contouring, highlight. A soft, gold color brushed right above cheekbones and into the hairline makes them more prominent. Dust a little down the center of your nose, and at the sides of temple.

If you're wearing a low-cut dress, a subtle dusting of gold shadow on collarbones and in between breasts creates a wonderful effect.

Now your palette is ready for the finishing touches. Give cheeks a hint of color. Then line lips. For a shimmery mouth, you may want to dab just a bit of bronze or other metallic color right in the center of lips, and blend to a gentle whisper.

To emphasize eyebrows, spritz a little hair spray onto eyebrow brush and brush brows upward. Your eyeshadow should complement your dress— except, of course, if the dress is white, an eyecolor which is too harsh for anyone to wear.

Just a hint of metallic color on eyes, perhaps right on browbone or in the center of the lower lid, is enough to transform eyes from evening to formal. Or sweep one soft color on the inner half of lid and crease, and a smoky shade on the other half right to the edge of the brow bone.

For more drama, use a pencil rather than a shadow to line outer edges just above eyelashes and underneath bottom rim just below lower lashes. Now is when you can "break" the rule and line inside lower lashes with blue pencil for totally mysterious eyes.

Top lashes with two or three coats of mascara. Use brow comb to feather and separate them in between mascara applications.

If lashes are short or thin, false eyelashes may be just what you need. They're perfect for that glamorous look, as long as they are not too thick so that they look artificial. Once you've glued them on, one coat of mascara over both natural and false eyelashes is enough. Never, *never* sleep without removing false lashes and mascara!

Now, give face a final dusting of translucent powder. Avoid eye area. You don't want powder on those lashes!

PROFESSIONAL LESSON

Of course, the best way to learn how to apply makeup, or how to update your look, is to have your face done professionally. It's a one-time expense that can pay off handsomely. And knowing what works best for you means you can pare down your cosmetics to the bare minimum.

But, since a professional makeover is not a reality for most, the step-by-step makeovers in the eight-page color section are designed to answer many of your questions. These pages are the best proof that a picture is worth a thousand words.

Naima's makeover demonstrates that minimal makeup works for *sport.* And just a few of the right touches for her orange undertones transforms her look into *daytime* and *business.*

Then, a step-by-step makeover of Mrs. Anna Velasquez, who has yellow undertones, incorporates all the basics of makeup application, showing how a beautiful woman can become absolutely glamorous for *evening.*

The final makeover demonstrates that with a dramatic weight loss and the right makeup, haircut and style, a totally new woman can emerge. Juanda Green is the best testimony that feeling good means looking good! Her confidence radiates and is guaranteed to inspire even the biggest doubter. Juanda has yellow undertones, and her makeover is designed for that fabulous *formal* occasion.

FINISHING TOUCHES

A spritz of fragrance, pretty hands and polished toenails are beauty's finishing touches. Paying close attention to these incidentals is as personal as adding your signature to a love letter.

SCENT-UOUS . . . SCENT-SATIONAL!

The aromatic pleasures of fragrance—a ritual which began with the ancient Egyptians—soothes the body and calms the psyche. Enveloping yourself from head-to-toe in a total scent-uous experience is refreshing, invigorating, tantalizing.

Bath oils, body lotions and perfumes are simple, yet exquisite, ways to make you feel pampered and smell scent-sational.

"Fragrance should be applied all over the body, from the feet up," says Annette Green, executive director of the Fragrance Foundation in New York City.

Why is body layering so important? "Fragrance rises. If a woman applies her fragrance just behind her ears, the scent will quickly evaporate."

THE BATH

The bath is where fragrance layering begins. Oils poured into bath water gently veil the skin, sealing in moisture while adding soft, velvety texture. Salts and crystals soften the water in addition to adding fragrant color, but sensitive skin can react adversely to these, as well as to some perfume-rich soaps or gels.

Very hot water, no matter how tempting, dehydrates skin. Warm-to-the-touch bathwater is best for both skin and relaxation, but keep soaks short for optimum benefits.

During your bath, gently buff body with a loofah, the earth's natural sponge, to remove dead skin cells and keep you all-over touchable. A cold-water finish closes pores, stimulates circulation.

After patting skin until it's moist, begin the next aromatic layer by massaging your favorite perfumed body lotion everywhere—including buttocks, elbows, heels. Puff with scented powder for a smooth finish.

Then, says Annette, "To layer with fragrance, start with a neck-to-toe application of toilet water. Follow with perfume applied at pulse points—behind ears, nape of neck, bosom, bend of elbows, wrists, behind knees, and at ankles—areas where the pulse of the heartbeat is closest to the surface of the skin. The heat generated at these points intensifies a perfume's impact."

Perfume is stronger and more concentrated than toilet water. And toilet water is stronger than cologne, the lightest form of fragrance. Don't expect perfume to last all day. It should be refreshed periodically. Here's a personal tip to help perfume last longer, longest.

Just before spritzing, apply a cream in the same fragrance as your perfume directly onto the area where you will put your perfume. This forms a "barrier" that prevents your body's natural oils from mixing with the oils in your fragrance. Now, apply perfume directly onto cream. The result? Scent remains truer!

PRECIOUS NAILS

Pretty nails are precious nails! That's what licensed cosmetologist Vita Fields, proprietor of Precious Nails, Inc., in Los Angeles, believes.

"When you meet a friend, what you usually do first is to extend your hand," she says, "so your nails should be as beautiful as you are."

In nail care, it's the little things like shape and polish that count. "Avoid shaping nails with any metal implement," says Vita, "because it causes nails to fray. And use a very good base coat so that polish will not bleed down into, or damage, the matrix."

The matrix is the area one fourth of an inch behind the cuticle. Sometimes called the mother nail, it's the place from which nails grow.

"That's why it's so important not to impair the cuticle by cutting it, or glueing it down to the body of the nail," Vita cautions. "Plus, cutting makes cuticles grow back tougher. Instead, gently push them back and only clip hangnails."

Women with soft nails should not use any vitamin E oil on them, warns Vita. "Vitamin E causes nails to split and slough away from the bed. Use vitamin E only if your nails are dry and brittle."

When it comes to polish, it's not imperative that nail color exactly match

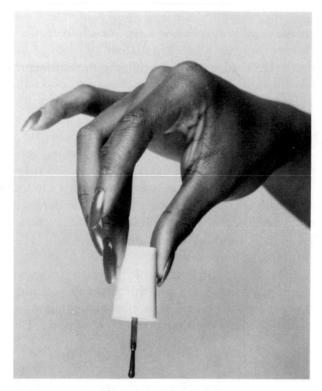

Photo: Vince Frye

cheek and lip color. But the color for nails should be in the same family as colors for cheeks and lips.

Pale nails that are well-shaped and healthy-looking are the solution for busy women on the go. Worries over telltale, chipped polish are eliminated when healthy nails go clear. However, do polish with a base coat first, then top with clear polish. Or forgo polish altogether and buff for natural shine.

The French manicure—clear nails that have white polished tips—makes a fashion statement. Since the color never clashes with what you're wearing, your nails are ready whenever you are.

Rather than using a pale pink top coat, ask your manicurist for a soft beige polish. It's a better blend with our skin color.

Vita believes that for the best manicure you should go to the professionals. "Many women make the mistake of cutting where they shouldn't, and this causes a lot of damage to delicate nail tissue."

But for the times when you just can't get to the pro, here are my basic steps to an at-home manicure.

A Basic Manicure:

- Remove old polish.
- Using the coarse side of an emery board, file tips of nails into smooth, oval shapes, not squares or unnatural points. To prevent breakage, file with light strokes in one direction only.
- Soak fingertips in sudsy water or in a hot nail oil-treatment for five minutes. Scrub nails on top and underneath with a soft nail brush. · With the end of a nail file, remove any remaining dirt from underneath nails. Resoak five minutes. Dry hands and apply cuticle remover to base and sides of nails.
- Do not cut cuticles. Instead, gently nudge cuticles back with a cotton-covered orangewood stick. Use a professional cuticle clipper to cut hangnails *only.*
- This step calls for a nail-buffing kit. Or you can substitute with an emery board to remove ridges and smooth nail surface, then use a chamois cloth to buff nails. Buff each nail about thirty times in one direction only. If your kit comes with a buffing paste, the paste will moisturize nails and give them a lustrous, healthy finish. Brush nails with soap and water to remove paste. Massage with a moisturizing hand lotion.
- You will not need to buff every time you manicure. Once every two weeks should keep your nails well stimulated. And the smoother surface will help nail polish adhere longer.
- Before applying polish, use a base coat. It helps prevent polish from staining nails. Then apply two coats of color and let nails dry just a bit—at least four minutes—before applying a clear top coat to seal and protect polish.
- After nails dry, dip a cotton swab in remover and whisk excess polish from sides of nails.

PLASTIC TIPS

Any woman who wants long, healthy nails can have them! Plastic tips are the newest way to have pretty hands.

At Classy Nail in Los Angeles, tips are glued onto the upper third of your natural nail. Silk and linen wraps give a smooth, protective finish that allows nails to "breathe."

Tips are so easy-to-wear and natural-looking that even with a French manicure, it's impossible to tell the difference!

SCULPTURED NAILS

It's a rescue for the chronic nail-biter, or the woman whose nails continue to split and break. But wearing sculptured nails for too long causes your own nails to become rubbery soft and thinly frail.

When it comes to sculptured nails, which is better—porcelain or acrylic?

"Porcelain nails are harder, more durable," says Vita. "But if you break porcelain, the break goes right down to your natural nail. On the other hand, acrylic does not last as long and won't endure heat or pressure. If you break acrylic, though, it will not damage your natural nail. The choice is up to the individual, but remember that any chemical put onto the nail changes the nail."

Nail length says a lot about style, and fashionable nails should be kept to a reasonable length. If too long, nails look artificial and unattractive. Remember, moderation is one rule that's always in style.

Here are some commonsense tips from Precious Nails to help you keep your sculptured nails in great shape:

- *Use a pencil or pen to dial or push buttons on phone.*
- *Don't try to remove tabs on beverage cans.*
- *Don't try to repair nail cracks and breaks yourself.*
- *Change polish once a week.*
- *Never shake or stir nail polish. It causes air bubbles. To mix, roll bottle between hands.*

SOFT HANDS

Just as good nail care is a way of life, so, too, is caring for hands. "They should be massaged with a moisturizing hand lotion every time hands leave water," says Vita.

And she adds this surprising tip: don't use rubber gloves. "Rubber gloves are not designed for fingernails. They are made to protect hands."

What about ruining nails in water? "If you wear a topcoat or bonder, nails are sealed and polish won't come off just because you're washing dishes. If it does, that means it's time to strip and repolish your nails."

If you do wear gloves, replace them often. And be sure to turn them inside-out after every use so they can dry and be exposed to sunlight. This kills any bacteria that the fleece lining may harbor.

FOOT WORK

Feet need work and attention, too. Keeping them soft and well-groomed is a daily task which begins right in the tub.

"Every time you step into a shower or take a bath, you should gently pumice your feet," insists Vita. Pumice, not cutting, is still the best way to remove dead skin and calluses. But don't overdo. Some amount of callus is necessary to protect feet when you walk.

The time of year dictates how often you'll need a pedicure. If you're wearing boots during the winter, pedicure about once every two to three weeks. In summer, pedicure every two weeks, especially if you're wearing sandals. Here are some additional tips:

- Use a clipper to cut nails straight across, then smooth tips with an emery board.
- Soak feet ten minutes.
- Smooth heels and soles with pumice stone.
- Fold tissues lengthwise and weave in and out of toes to separate them before applying polish.

NEW SHOES

No matter how attractive or how great a bargain, tight shoes are murder on feet. And one good way to ruin your toes is by trying to break in shoes after you buy them. New shoes should immediately feel comfortable, right in the store. Remember: smart walking shoes—or running shoes—are always in style!

If you have any serious foot problems, see a podiatrist. Be good to your feet. After all, they're your pedestal!

Special Effects

SOMETHING EXTRA

In this section, I offer you a little something extra. Here are a few beauty bonuses, just for you.

Every woman wants to be as beautiful as possible on her wedding day. "Bridal Beauty" is filled with tips you will need so that your walk down the aisle is every bit as memorable as it should be.

If you're expecting a baby, you'll want to look and feel your best during and after your pregnancy. The information in "The Two of Us" discusses the importance of prenatal care, proper weight gain and moderate exercise.

Next comes "Breast Appeal." Breast size is addressed, and more importantly, breast health is stressed. How to examine your breasts for optimum health is a focal point here.

Women over fifty have special beauty concerns, too, and "At Your Age" is designed to ensure that your lifetime investment of sensible habits collects enough interest to earn you real dividends!

"Extra Senses" puts the spotlight on women who are handicap-*able.* Since people tend to pay more attention when they see a wheelchair, why not give them something pretty to look at? A former model tells why she takes extra time out for her hair and skin, especially now that she sees the world from a *different* point of view.

Since who you are *inside* is what is seen *outside,* leading psychologist Alvin Poussaint, Ph.D., discusses why beauty is important to the opposite sex. And Minnie Claiborne, Ph.D., offers her priceless keys to unlock the doors of self-esteem. It's all in the chapter "Sensuality."

Remember, beauty is also in the heart, mind and spirit. How well you fine-tune that instrument called *you* determines how feminine—and sexy—you really are!

BRIDAL BEAUTY

Finally, your wedding day is here! It's a day you've dreamed about—a time you've anticipated. Here's how to make your bridal beauty as romantic as the moment that you say, "I do!"

TIMES TO REMEMBER

The wedding day is just one of those times to highlight in the album of your life. Proms, dinner parties, sorority events and formal affairs are also gala occasions.

Although this chapter focuses on the bride, there are tips here that you'll want to treasure for these other times as well. It's all designed so that your reflections will be tender memories to last a lifetime.

For your celebration, you'll want to add a glorious touch to everything you do—the way you style your hair . . . the way you apply your makeup. Once dressed, the right posture helps you to stand as pretty as you look.

A GOOD NIGHT

Your beauty preparation actually begins long before that special day arrives. You'll want to be so organized that you've completed all those last-minute details that can leave the bride-to-be frazzled and exhausted.

The day before the wedding should be time that's all yours. Pamper yourself with a shampoo and set, manicure and pedicure the day before. If there's room in the budget, why not indulge in a professional body massage?

Afterward, a brisk, late-afternoon walk can help you ease body and mind as you reflect on the time ahead. Avoid vigorous aerobic exercise, especially close to bedtime. It can wake your body up rather than calm you down.

Probably your most important—and difficult task—will be to sneak away somewhere peaceful for a good night's sleep. Perhaps your grandmother, favorite aunt or special friend can seclude you from excited bridesmaids, family and friends and offer her quiet home just for you.

Or check into a hotel the night before the wedding. It can even be the same one where you plan to spend your wedding night so that all you have to do is join your husband in your marriage suite.

Whatever your choice, once in your haven, a wonderful warm bath is the perfect relaxant. Use bath oils to pamper your skin so that it is gloriously soft.

STAYING DRY

With all the excitement, it'll be a challenge not to perspire on wedding day. One day before, remove underarm hairs to help check odor.

The night before, apply antiperspirant just before retiring. Then reapply after your morning shower. Dust generously with powder. Even with these precautions, it's still a good idea to wear dress shields to protect your dress.

For the woman who really wants to splurge, a complete body waxing will remove every trace of hair. And because waxing *epiabrades*—removes old skin cells—a new, fresh layer of skin will make you feel incredibly touchable.

Lydia Safarti of Sarkli/Repêchage Ltd. in New York recommends waxing a small area at a time to minimize sensitivity. "And," she cautions, "don't wait until your wedding to be waxed for the first time. This is not the time to experiment."

THE ELEGANT STYLE

Because the elegant style is a simple one, your hair should be the least of your worries. Here are a few tips from Clifford Peterson of Clifford's on Rodeo Drive in Beverly Hills.

"The best rule is to stick with what's traditional," advises Clifford. "This is not the time to try to be original or to try to make a statement. Simplicity is impeccably stylish. It's the trademark of the truly sophisticated woman."

Clifford personally styled singer Diana Ross's hair for her wedding day. What was the wise solution? Diana's hair was combed off the face and secured at the nape with a chignon.

In general, follow this rule: Wedding-day hair should be styled "up." The veil actually takes the place of your "hair." The addition of jewelry plus

Photo: Carrie Branovan. Hair by Gianni Lonnro, Smith and Lonnro, London. Reprinted from Bride's *magazine. Copyright © 1987 Condé Nast Publications, Inc.*

the detail from your dress should not have to compete with a long hairstyle.

A simple hairstyle not only works best for any special occasion, but it also eliminates worry of how your hair will hold up during the event. These photos from *Bride's* magazine are perfect examples of the ideal bridal hairstyle.

FLAWLESS MAKEUP

Top fashion model Iman understands the importance of flawless makeup that lasts all day yet looks as fresh as when it was first applied. Here are a few of her personal "secrets."

For pale, sensuous lips, cover them first with a foundation base that's just a tone darker than your skin. The foundation gives a matte finish and moisturizes lips, too.

When it's time for powder, don't dust with a puff or brush, which gives thicker coverage. Dust a tissue with translucent powder. Lightly press it onto your face. The tissue will absorb excess moisture while pressing on just a little powder. Fold a powdered tissue into your purse for touch-ups.

Finally, a misty spray of mineral water gives you a fresh glow and "sets" makeup.

PERFECT POSTURE

Actress Olga Adderley believes that correct posture can make any woman feel as regal as a princess. She has studied the Alexander Technique and offers these suggestions for the perfect pose.

When standing, rather than arching your back and swinging buttocks and hips downward, try this: Hold in your tummy and tuck your pelvis upward, toward the front, rather than toward the floor.

To really get the feel of this Alexander Technique for posture, Olga suggests you stand with your back against the wall with heels twelve inches away from the wall. To make sure that your feet are the right distance, place a ruler on the floor so that one heel can touch the tip of the ruler.

Now, lower your shoulders and tuck your pelvis under so that your shoulders, middle back and buttocks are touching the wall. Your knees will be slightly bent.

Pretend that there's a string from the middle of your head giving you a nice long line. Keep eyes and chin level. Think about what's happening to

Photo of model Iman by Eric Bowman. Reprinted from Bride's *magazine. Copyright © 1986 Condé Nast Publications, Inc.*

your body and try to remember how correct posture feels. It's probably very different from the way you're used to standing.

After you're aligned against the wall and there's no space between your body and the wall, walk "up" the wall, bringing your feet as close to the wall as you possibly can.

Do not leave the wall at all or disturb the alignment. Your knees should still be slightly bent. Push away from the wall holding this alignment.

Now, imagine that your tailbone in the back and your pelvic bone to the front left and right form a three-legged stool. Walk heel-to-toe.

"It may feel a little awkward at first," says Olga, "but you will have to remind yourself throughout the day to stand correctly until it becomes a habit. When you're standing on line at the bank or waiting for a light at the corner, think about the feeling of standing against the wall and consciously, deliberately realign yourself."

For perfect wedding-day posture, practice walking correctly several weeks before. Remember to always relax your shoulders. Pulling them up and back increases tension in the neck and chest as well as in the shoulders.

Well, now you've attended to every detail for your special day. All that's left for you to do is get to the church on time!

THE TWO OF US

Now that there are *two* of you, taking care of yourself from the inside out is an absolute must!

PRENATAL CARE

What a wonderful time to be pregnant! Women are taking better care of themselves, continuing their educations, furthering their careers and fulfilling life goals.

Doctors, with a positive approach to pregnancy, encourage women to continue to enjoy the activities which are a normal part of their lifestyle. And prenatal care is at its best, with the most advanced testing and health care available.

The importance of seeing an obstetrician from the earliest stages of pregnancy was highlighted in a recent study published by the University of Michigan.

The report, headed by Kristine A. Siefert, professor of social work, and Louise Doss-Martin, regional public health social work consultant with the U.S. Public Health Service, stressed this: health education and counseling, early pregnancy testing, nutritional assistance, and identification and treatment of high-risk patients contribute to a healthier mother and baby.

In addition to monitoring your pregnancy, your obstetrician can answer pertinent questions which are certain to arise during the course of your nine months. Although each woman's body is different and each pregnancy an individual experience, some of your major concerns are addressed here.

STRETCH MARKS

Women worry about stretch marks, and in dark complexions stretch marks can leave bothersome trails of hyperpigmentation.

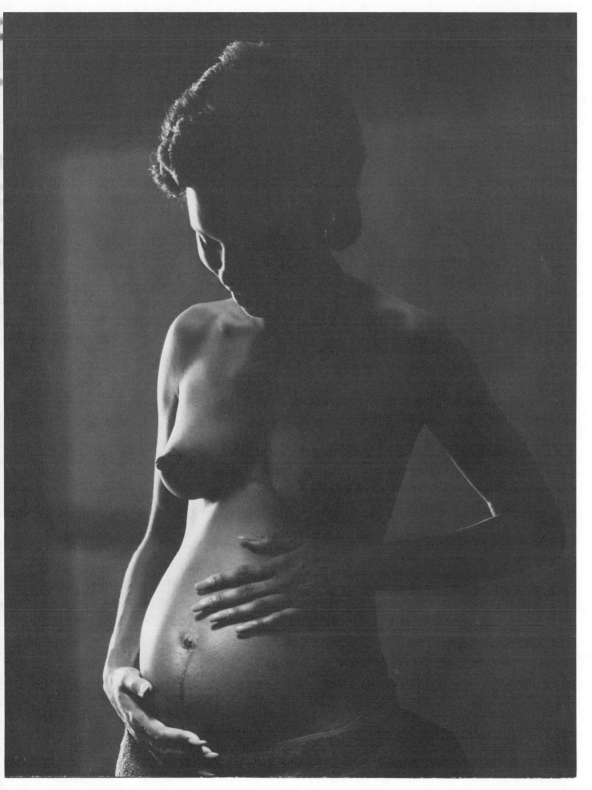

Photo: George Selman

"There's no formula to predict who will or who will not get stretch marks during pregnancy," says Vanessa A. Castine, M.D., an obstetician/gynecologist in private practice and on the staffs of Centinela Medical Center, Daniel Freeman Hospital and Robert F. Kennedy Medical Center in Los Angeles.

"It may be genetic. If your mother had stretch marks, the tendency for you may be increased, but this is just a theory."

According to clinical research, there's also no way to prevent stretch marks. They occur in areas where the skin—breasts, thighs, abdomen—has been stretched to the breaking point.

"Some women have perfect skin until the last day of their pregnancy. Then, with so much tension, their skin just stretches," notes Dr. Castine.

Many women believe that keeping the skin lubricated helps it to maintain moisture and flexibility, minimizing stretch marks. Again, this is unproven, but if gently massaging breasts, thighs, abdomen and stomach daily to lock in moisture doesn't actually help, it may increase relaxation, which is a pregnant plus.

THE MASK OF PREGNANCY

Just as the skin on the body may be affected by pregnancy, so, too, can the skin on face and neck. Called the mask of pregnancy, *chloasma* is hyperpigmented or dark areas which occur under the eyes, above upper lip, on cheeks, or neck. Because the skin in these areas can become up to three shades darker than normal, it looks as though there's a "mask" painted onto the surface of the skin.

Chloasma is stimulated by hormones which activate pigment cells. In Black women, chloasma often occurs on the neck and looks like a large, dark band.

If chloasma occurs during pregnancy, Dr. Castine advises staying out of bright sunlight and wearing moisturizers which contain sunscreen. Postpartum, chloasma generally disappears. However, in cases where it persists, patients are referred to dermatologists who may recommend hydroquinone or topical steroids.

HAIR GROWTH AND LOSS

Increased hair growth is usually welcomed during pregnancy, except when it occurs on the face and neck and around the ears.

"It looks like baby fuzz," says Dr. Castine, "and can be especially troublesome. The good news is that six to eight weeks postpartum, this extra hair completely disappears."

In fact, two to five months after delivery, women may complain of hair loss from the scalp. "Hair on the head has grown so nicely, then it tends to fall out postpartum. That's because it is rushed into the telogen phase."

Like everything else in life, hair goes through continuing cycles. A cycle begins with a four-year period of growth, called the *anagen* stage. The second is a transitional stage called the *catagen,* which lasts approximately one week. Finally, there is a resting stage or *telogen,* which lasts for nearly three months. Once the full cycle is complete, hair falls out.

Surgery, stress or high fever are all systemic insults which can rush hair into its telogen phase. Once past this phase, the hair will again grow normally.

"After pregnancy, think about trying a new haircut or wearing a different style," Dr. Castine suggests. "But for now, relax and don't worry about your hair."

WEIGHT GAIN

Nutrition takes on added importance when the body is working to feed two instead of one. During pregnancy, the temptation to indulge in every culinary fantasy weighs heavily. The resulting pounds can mean an uncomfortable pregnancy and slow postpartum weight loss.

Malverse Martin, M.D., an obstetrician on staff at the West Hills Medical Center in Los Angeles offers the following advice about weight gain: "Although weight gain depends upon each woman's height, weight and bone structure, a twenty-five-to-thirty-pound weight gain over the total course of the pregnancy is ideal."

How much should you eat?

"All the body needs to fulfill the nutritional demands of the fetus is an additional three hundred calories a day *above* what your normal intake would be to maintain an ideal body weight. That is the equivalent of an extra two glasses of milk."

Pregnancy is not the time to diet, but neither is it the time for total abandon. And Dr. Martin adds this incentive, "When weight gain is moderate, the chance of getting stretch marks is minimized."

KEEPING ACTIVE

Pregnancy is the time to keep active. But Dr. Castine advises against being too adventuresome, or embarking on a new sport during pregnancy.

"If you've never played tennis before, pregnancy is not the time to begin taking tennis lessons. The body is a bit more clumsy now, and ligaments, joints and tendons are a bit more lax. Injury is more common."

Although many active women continue with their regular routines throughout their nine months, even the athletic woman may find she gets pooped easily.

"Pregnancy displaces the diaphragm upward and lung volumn is decreased. You'll get a little winded because, when you take a deep breath, you're not getting quite as much air. Don't be surprised if the level of performance is not as high as it was before."

EXERCISE

Exercise helps monitor weight gain and, in addition, increases muscle flexibility. But what kind of exercise is best for the mother-to-be?

Dr. Castine recommends specific pregnancy-oriented exercise.

"Regular aerobics classes and nonpregnancy exercises don't take into consideration the body mechanics of pregnant women. Sit-ups to strengthen the abdominal muscles are inappropriate in pregnancy. And lifting weights can sometimes put too much pressure on the back."

Prenatal exercise focuses on developing those muscles you will need most during labor and childbirth. In most classes, women are also taught to practice proper breathing, which is good preparation for labor. Deep, cleansing breaths strengthen the abdominals and aid in relaxation and control. Stretching enhances breathing capacity.

And, says Dr. Castine, because a pregnant woman is more buoyant, swimming is another excellent exercise. Many muscle groups are used during this relaxing workout.

Before embarking on *any* exercise, it is imperative that, first, you check with your obstetrician. Each woman's body is different, and what may work for one may not necessarily benefit another. Discuss your program thoroughly with your physician to make certain it is absolutely safe for you and your baby.

Lisa Kingston is a certified fitness instructor and personal fitness trainer to many celebrities in Beverly Hills. She has a degree in physical education and served as a fitness consultant to Valley Presbyterian Hospital.

To gently tone and slowly stretch those muscle groups you'll need most during pregnancy and delivery, Lisa offers the following pregnancy exercises:

Abdomen and Lower Back

PELVIC TILT:
Lie on the floor with your knees bent, feet flat on the floor and shoulder-width apart. As you exhale, contract abdomen and buttocks muscles and tilt pelvis upward, keeping the small of your back pressed to the floor. Relax and return hips to the floor. This exercise should be done slowly. In latter months, rather than trying to get up and down, stand with knees bent, feet slightly apart and hands on what used to be your waist. Tilt pelvis upward and hold for a few seconds.

THE ELEVATOR:
Lie down. Contract your pelvic-floor muscles—those surrounding, urinary tract, vaginal and rectal area—as if you are trying to keep from urinating. Imagine your muscles in an elevator slowly going up to the second floor, then the third and the fourth. Relax.
Note: This exercise helps with incontinence and restores vaginal tightness for enjoyable intercourse postpartum.

Upper Back

SHOULDER ROLLS:
Sit comfortably in a chair. Slowly roll your shoulders backward. This helps alleviate upper-back tension caused by poor posture and heavier breasts.

Buttocks

BUT-TUCKS:
Begin with a standing pelvic tilt. Gently squeeze buttocks, hold for a few seconds, relax.

Feet

FOOT CIRCLES:
To stimulate blood flow back to the heart and discourage varicose veins, sit in a chair and gently rotate your feet at the ankles.

Lisa combines these exercises with a program of walking for her pregnant clients. Walking increases circulation and oxygen intake, and promotes a general feeling of well-being as you enjoy the outdoors.

The most important piece of equipment in walking is a pair of walking sneakers to aid with balance and body alignment.

"Think proper posture when you walk. As the abdomen thrusts forward, the tendency is to allow the back to sway. If you pay attention to proper posture throughout pregnancy, many aches and pains could be avoided," says Lisa.

ACOG GUIDELINES

The following guidelines are based on the unique physical and physiological conditions that exist during pregnancy and the postpartum period. They outline general criteria for safety to provide direction to patients in the development of home exercise programs.

Pregnancy and Postpartum

1. Regular exercise (at least three times a week) is preferable to intermittent activity. Competitive activities should be discouraged.
2. Vigorous exercise should not be performed in hot, humid weather or during a period of febrile illness.
3. Ballistic movements (jerky, bouncy motions) should be avoided. Exercise should be done on a wooden floor or a tightly carpeted surface to reduce shock and provide a sure footing.
4. Deep flexion or extension of joints should be avoided because of connective tissue laxity. Activities that require jumping, jarring motions or rapid changes in direction should be avoided because of joint instability.
5. Vigorous exercise should be preceded by a five-minute period of muscle warm-up. This can be accomplished by slow walking or stationary cycling with low resistance.
6. Vigorous exercise should be followed by a period of gradually declining activity that includes gentle stationary stretching. Because connective tissue laxity increases the risk of joint injury, stretches should not be taken to the point of maximum resistance.
7. Heart rate should be measured at times of peak activity. Target heart rates and limits established in consultation with the physician should not be exceeded.
8. Care should be taken to gradually rise from the floor to avoid

orthostatic hypotension. Some form of activity involving the legs should be continued for a brief period.

9.   Liquids should be taken liberally before and after exercise to prevent dehydration. If necessary, activity should be interrupted to replenish fluids.

10. Women who have led sedentary lifestyles should begin with physical activity of very low intensity and advance activity levels very gradually.

11. Activity should be stopped and the physician consulted if any unusual symptoms appear.

Reprinted with permission from the American College of Obstetricians and Gynecologists: Exercise During Pregnancy and Postnatal Period (ACOG Home Exercise Programs). Washington, D.C., ACOG, 1985.

OVER THIRTY-FIVE

More and more women are opting to delay motherhood until their late thirties or early forties. Good nutritional habits and healthy bodies take much of the worry out of waiting.

In fact, a report from the American College of Obstetrics and Gynecology says that a healthy thirty-five-year old, or older, can look forward to as safe a pregnancy and as healthy an infant as a woman in her early twenties.

And when compared with a teenage mother, the woman over thirty-five has these factors in her favor: she is more likely to be consistent with prenatal and neonatal care; she is more likely to give birth to a baby of normal weight.

Emotionally, the mature mother is likely to be more satisfied with herself since she's enjoyed the challenges of her career and experienced the benefits of a successful lifestyle. Her baby, the new career challenge, now shares—and creates—the rewards.

So if you find yourself fretting because the biological clock is ticking, remember that over thirty-five, or over forty, is not too late to have a baby. In fact, it's right on time!

A BLESSING

A good, positive outlook is so important during your pregnancy. Psychologists are studying this, but you'll probably have a baby who is more peaceful, calmer and easier to handle if you think good thoughts.

Pregnancy is a beautiful experience. It's a blessing to be able to have a child!

BREAST APPEAL

Toned muscles and body definition are benefits which show up front. As shoulders and upper arms are exercised, breast-framing pectoral muscles are also strengthened, improving bosom shape and appearance. Yes, breast appeal is important. But breast *health* should be our major concern.

IS BIGGER BETTER?

Many women feel that large, firm breasts are what most men consider to be sexy. When it comes to this feminine characteristic, the myth that bigger must certainly be better still exists.

Sex therapist Meredith Sirmans, M.D., medical director of Medical Services for Women in New York City, disagrees. He feels that symmetry, not size, is what appeals to men most.

"Proportion is the major factor in breast appeal," he explains, "and symmetry can be controlled by exercise which strengthens the underlying muscles. Genetics play a major role, but exercise is also a contributing factor."

Hormones determine the size of the fatty tissue, or mammary glands, called breasts. Heavy, pendulous breasts are high in *fatty* tissue and tend to feel soft. Breasts are strong and firm when the proportion of *fibrous* tissue is high. Shape and texture are also determined by menstruation, breast-feeding and body weight.

Except for very tiny muscles in the nipples, there are no muscles in the breasts. Instead, breasts lie on top of and are attached to pectoral, or chest, muscles, which extend to the upper arm and shoulder. So while exercise can help firm, it will not affect breast fullness.

Photo: George Selman

BREAST HEALTH

What should concern women most, Dr. Sirmans feels, is not breast size but breast health.

"This is the most important issue. Many Black women do not practice breast self-examination on a regular basis. They feel that if there is a problem they will feel pain, but breast cancer does not usually cause a woman pain until the cancer is quite advanced. By then, it's usually very late."

Stressing that a lump does not have to hurt before it's serious, Dr. Sirmans is concerned that many Black women delay early diagnosis and treatment simply because they are looking for the wrong symptoms.

"Pain, tenderness and a major degree of discomfort are *not* symptoms of *early* breast cancer."

BLACK WOMEN UNDER FORTY

Until a recent study headed by Claudia R. Baquet, M.D., M.P.H., minority field program director at the National Cancer Institute in Bethesda, Maryland, breast cancer was thought to be a disease which primarily affected older white women. But breast cancer is also a concern for Black women under age forty.

Says Dr. Baquet, "Studies to date have had only limited involvement of younger Black women. More is known about postmenopausal breast cancer."

Why is it important for young Black women to be on the breast-cancer alert?

"If the possibility of cancer is not even suspected in a particular age group, women and their physicians are less aggressive in determining whether or not breast cancer is, indeed, a fact. Black women under forty should be encouraged to practice breast self-examination and get mammograms and early treatment."

Pessimistic attitudes influence early diagnosis and treatment.

"Many Black women feel that breast cancer is fatal, so if they suspect a problem they convince themselves to accept it," says Dr. Baquet. "They may be unaware that varying degrees of surgery, radiation and rehabilitation can help maintain a quality and fulfilling life."

Additionally, the question of whether the lack of media programs directed to and involving Black women contributes to the fact that as a group we are not as aware of cancer's symptoms deserves consideration. Will it take more Blacks in advertising to impress upon Black women that breast cancer is an important concern?

GENERAL RISK FACTORS

There are general risk factors for breast cancer which Dr. Baquet feels every woman should know. These include genetics, reproductive factors and diet.

"Women with breast cancer in a first-degree relative—mother or sister —are at higher risk of developing breast cancer. Women who begin menstruation very early are at higher risk. Also, women who have their first child after age thirty-five, or who reach menopause later than others, are at increased risk."

In postmenopausal women, obesity is moderately associated with breast cancer. The amount of fat intake may be related, but proving this still requires more research.

Dr. Alfred Haynes, dean of Drew Postgraduate Medical School in Los Angeles and consultant to the U.S. Preventive Services Task Force Review Board, says, "Even though the evidence is not as firm as we would like, it does suggest that just as fiber is important in the diet, especially as it relates to colon cancer, it is important to eliminate fat from the diet, especially as it relates to breast cancer."

If a woman is at particular risk, she should inform her doctor so that she can be examined and evaluated on a regular basis. And since 80 percent of lumps are detected by women themselves, knowing how to properly detect breast lumps through breast self-examination means early treatment, which may save a breast—and a life.

BREAST SELF-EXAMINATION

Melvin A. Silverstein, M.D., is medical director of The Breast Center, a multidisciplinary health-care facility in Van Nuys, California. An average of three thousand women are screened annually by a staff which includes surgical, medical and radiation oncologists, a diagnostic radiologist, reconstructive surgeon, pathologist and psychiatrists.

Dr. Silverstein says breast self-examination, or BSE, allows *you* to be the first to notice any abnormality. By checking for lumps regularly, a woman will learn what feels normal.

He suggests practicing BSE preferably one week after menstruation or, for women who are postmenstrual, on the same day of every month. Choose the first of the month, because it's easy to remember.

According to Dr. Silverstein, there are two reasons women don't self-examine regularly.

"First, women fear they will actually find something and they'd rather not know. Secondly, because breasts may be lumpy to begin with, women feel that they will not be able to tell if anything is wrong, so why bother."

But, he explains, the purpose of monthly breast self-examination is this: "A woman who begins BSE at age twenty will, by age forty, have examined her breasts 240 times. She is now the expert and knows what is normal for her. If there is any change in the skin, nipple or texture of the breast it will be obvious to her first. And if there's a lump, she will probably find it two or three years earlier than it might have ordinarily been found."

The benefits, he explains, stack up in her favor. "Should there be a malignancy, she is early enough for *breast conservation,* a medical term for the saving of her breast. Most importantly, her life will be saved because she found the cancer in time. Waiting does not increase the chance that the lump will disappear, but it may increase the chance that it will grow larger."

Improved techniques in therapy and surgical procedures combined with early detection of breast cancer are a positive formula for breast health.

Remember, not every lump is malignant, and not every malignancy means mastectomy. The catchword in the medical community is "conservation," which means surgery is not always the first and only choice.

The American Cancer Society offers these simple steps for monthly breast self-examination:

Mirror Check

Stand in front of a mirror with arms resting at sides. Take a good look for any pigment changes, redness, discoloration or swelling. Next, lift arms above head and check for any unusual changes in size or shape of breast. Put hands on hips, press down and look again. Are there any scaly areas or sores on the nipple?

Clock Exam

Lie down with a small pillow or folded towel under your right shoulder. Lift right arm above head so that your shoulder is raised high. Place your right hand under your head, elbow resting on the bed. This position centers your breast on your chest and evenly distributes the tissues across the chest wall.

Using your left hand, keep fingers flat and together. Because fingertips are not as sensitive, use the entire surface of your fingers. Imagine there is a face of a clock on your breast with the times from 12, 1, 2, 3, all the way back to 12, evenly spaced around the perimeter.

Beginning clockwise and in a large circle at the outer circumference of breast, gently press, or *palpate*, breast until you have circled from 12:00 back to 12:00.

Begin again, moving this time an inch closer to the nipple. Gently press from 12:00 around to 12:00. The next circle should be even smaller and closer to the nipple.

Repeat for a total of at least four clockwise circles until the entire breast has been examined. Finally, squeeze the nipple to see if there is any discharge.

Repeat the entire procedure for the left breast, shifting the pillow under the left shoulder and resting the raised left arm under your head.

Do:

- *press gently but firmly to roll skin over underlying tissue and not just hand over skin.*
- *examine entire area including lymph nodes, collarbone and armpits.*
- *take note of a change which occurs in one breast but not the other.*
- *report any clear or bloody discharge to your doctor immediately.*

Don't:

- *press breasts between thumb and fingers. This creates a "lump."*
- *panic. Not every lump means cancer, but do make an appointment to see your doctor immediately.*
- *delay. Waiting prolongs your worry and time is essential if you do need special attention.*

MAMMOGRAPHY

Mammography, a low-dose X-ray procedure, discovers small tumors at their earliest stages. In fact, the detailed picture is so sensitive it can detect breast cancer as early as two years before it can be felt during BSE.

Of all the screening techniques available, mammography is the single most reliable. Monthly breast self-examination plus mammography and clinical examination of breasts reduce the cancer death rate by 30 percent.

The American Cancer Society suggests that every women over thirty-five have a mammogram. Depending on the family history and risk factors, women forty to forty-nine should have a mammogram every year or at the least, every other year. Once over fifty, a mammogram is recommended once a year.

Knowing what to expect during the quick, easy mammogram can help reduce fear of the unknown. The technique described here is what a woman might experience during a visit at a center like The Breast Center.

First, a brief medical history is taken on a standard form. Next, a woman is ushered into a small, private room and asked to disrobe to the waist, removing blouse, slip and bra.

Standing in front of the X-ray machine, breasts are compressed between plastic sheets so that they are as "flat" as possible. Compression is important because it allows the breast tissue to be spread so that minute details can be detected. This procedure requires that the technician gently press each breast for an accurate picture.

Most women feel no discomfort with updated equipment but sensitivity varies from woman to woman. It takes only a few seconds for the mammogram to be completed, so even if there is tenderness the overall procedure is quite brief.

Two types of mammogram are *film screen* and *Xerox.* "In our opinion, film screen is far superior," says Dr. Silverstein. "Though a little more expensive than Xerox, film screen is state-of-the-art. It uses a lower dose of radiation and allows the soft tissues to be seen more accurately."

Ask which type will be used for your mammography.

BIOPSY

For further examination if a lump is discovered, *biopsy* is a surgical procedure during which a piece of tissue is removed to be examined under the microscope.

Biopsy determines the exact nature of that particular area of the breast and because the amount of tissue usually involves only a small area, the biopsy should not cosmetically disfigure.

However, some Black women have a medical history of forming *hypertrophic* scars, a slightly raised and darkened scar that heals incorrectly. If a biopsy is recommended, the physician should be alerted prior to the procedure so that he or she is aware of this tendency.

Women with a familial or personal history of *keloidal* scarring, that piling up of scar tissue into a large, shiny growth, should also inform their physician.

Before agreeing to a biopsy, get a second opinion. But don't use this as a subtle excuse to avoid the procedure altogether. See another doctor immediately and don't delay.

Dr. Silverstein advises that since most biopsies are performed under local anesthesia, they need only be performed on an outpatient basis.

"Try to resist going into the hospital for what will take approximately one hour. Spending the night in a hospital is not only more time-consuming, it's more expensive as well."

Additionally, he cautions *never* to sign approval for a biopsy and mastectomy in one stage. "Sign for biopsy only. If there is a problem, evaluate all the alternatives before agreeing to a mastectomy."

MODIFIED MASTECTOMY

Today, a *modified* mastectomy replaces the *radical* mastectomy in many cases. The former involves removal of the entire breast and adjacent lymph nodes in the armpit. But underlying tissues are not removed so that reconstructive surgery is almost always possible.

Techniques for reconstruction—surgically rebuilding the breast with implants—can close the chapter on a painful experience and make a woman feel whole again.

The benefits of reconstruction are primarily emotional. Women find that with a greater range in clothing selection, they are less likely to focus on the past illness.

LUMPECTOMY

A less traumatic surgery, *lumpectomy,* followed by radiation therapy, does not require removal of the breast. Under some circumstances, lumpectomy, in which the lump is excised along with a surrounding margin of healthy tissue, is reported to provide the same success rates as mastectomy.

However, because size of the lump and its location are major factors, lumpectomy must be performed in the early stages and is yet another encouragement to see a doctor at the first signs of a tumor.

Before making any decision, research and be sure you have sufficient information. Three qualified opinions allow you to exercise all your options.

It's your body, so be diligent to get the care you deserve.

TOLL-FREE NUMBER

You might want to keep this toll-free phone number handy. The National Cancer Institute answers questions and provides free literature. Call 1-800-4-CANCER.

Free literature is also available by writing the American Cancer Society in your area. Check the listing in your phone book.

Photo: George Selman

AT YOUR AGE

At your age, you not only look fabulous, you *are!* Isn't this proof that a lifetime of good health and beauty habits pays?

Over fifty, you're probably busier than ever, but now is when you should devote more time to you. Even if your schedule doesn't allow it, carving out personal hours in the day for play should be your first priority.

YOU'RE MORE SECURE

Now that you have a better grip on life and feel secure with who you are, it seems almost unfair that, without giving you notice or receiving your permission, your body changes. The plusses, however, stack high in favor of that quality we call maturity.

But what's addressed here is the little minuses. While it's impossible to stop the clock altogether, there are precautions you can take so that these years are truly your best—even during menopause.

MENOPAUSE

Younger women are often baffled when they hear talk of those hot flashes which hit at around age forty-five to fifty-five. But *menopause,* or change of life, is one inevitable result of aging every woman experiences to some degree.

Hot flashes, or "sweats," are menopause's early symptoms. A flushed feeling of heat in the area from head to chest, coupled with perspiration, causes great anxiety in some women.

Additionally, irritability, nervousness, depression, forgetfulness and crying spells can place the menopausal woman on an emotional roller coaster.

A positive attitude can help determine whether or not menopause will be traumatic for you, or whether it will be just another of life's natural transitions. Although a good outlook can help to some degree, your body *is* losing an important hormone—estrogen.

ESTROGEN

Estrogen and *progesterone* are essential hormones in the emotional balance and physical appearance of women.

With age, the ovaries gradually decrease production of estrogen, signaling the end of menstruation and the reproductive years. Sometimes menstruation stops all at once; sometimes it becomes erratic and gradually tapers to a halt.

It is the loss of estrogen which propels the body into menopause. Depending on the woman, symptoms of menopause can range from relatively few to a combination of symptoms including vaginal dryness, muscle, joint and back aches, palpitations or insomnia.

Understanding that your body is changing is perhaps the best help you can give yourself. And enlisting the support of your family and friends can ease the pressure of being misunderstood.

Besides that, seek your doctor's help. Estrogen-replacement therapy, ERT—which puts estrogen back into the body—is reportedly one successful way to help ease the severe effects of menopause.

In addition to psychological changes in the menopausal to postmenopausal stages, physical changes occur. What's discussed here is how body, skin and hair can react to the loss of estrogen.

OSTEOPOROSIS

As some women age, their spine shortens. Bones become a little more brittle and there seems to be a constant battle of the bulge, especially in the stomach and thigh areas.

In women who are affected, *osteoporosis* occurs after menopause due, in part, to an estrogen deficiency. Osteoporosis, loss of calcium or bone density, weakens the spinal vertebrae, causing loss of height, inward curvature of the upper spine, pain, fractures and protrusion of the abdomen.

When bones lose calcium, tiny holes leave them weak and brittle. By age eighty, the vertebrae, especially the portion in the upper back, curves into a "dowager's hump." Hips and wrists also become fragile.

As the back loses inches, the belly has less area over which to stretch. Now, the same amount of flesh is compacted into a smaller space, reduced because of spinal shrinkage. Women who may never have had this concern in their younger years find they are suddenly dealing with a persistent, protruding tummy.

CALCIUM SUPPLEMENTS

If the body's *calcium* reserve is low, it borrows from bones which contain 98 percent of the body's supply. *Periodontal disease* may be an early indication of a calcium deficiency.

Although osteoporosis results from long-term calcium deficiency, calcium supplements, taken in moderation, may be a plus for the woman over fifty.

The National Institutes of Health suggest 1,000 milligrams of calcium for middle-aged women who still have estrogen and 1,500 milligrams of calcium for postmenopausal women who are not on estrogen therapy.

Before taking any supplement, check with your doctor. Some women may be hyperabsorbers of calcium and should avoid taking any. Women with kidney stones should not take calcium either, because although calcium does not cause kidney stones, it is a contributing factor in the disease.

Excellent calcium food sources, of course, are dairy products—milk, cheese, yogurt. Egg yolks, tofu, molasses, sardines, almonds, sesame seeds, Brussels sprouts, collards and turnip greens are also calcium-rich.

Alcohol and nicotine are calcium thieves and health robbers. Vitamins D, A and C improve calcium absorption.

So, too, does exercise. In addition to aiding muscle tone, exercise encourages bone density.

STRETCH AND TONE

Exercises which stretch the back and tone the abdominals will help keep you trim. You may have to work out a little more than you did five or ten years ago, but consistency is key in maintaining muscle tone.

Back-stretching exercises encourage elongation. And those sit-ups you took for granted to help keep your abdomen firm are a must now.

In general, active women have tougher, healthier bones than women who do not exercise regularly. You don't have to become an aerobics enthusiast, but moderate, daily workouts are like best friends to your body.

Walking, jogging, bicycling, jumping rope, tennis and golf all increase the flow of oxygen, which clinicians believe is as important for bones and joints as calcium. Runners experience less arthritis and have fewer disabilities. Best of all, they enjoy better overall health.

And your thighs will love the workout!

SKIN CARE

As important as calcium is to bones, *collagen* is to skin.

Called the "glue" of skin, collagen—fibrous protein for connective tissue—helps hold skin together so that it retains elasticity. Like an old rubber band that has lost its snap, skin sags and wrinkles with the loss of collagen.

The *dermis,* the second layer of skin, is below the three layers of the *epidermis,* the outermost portion of skin. It is here, in the dermis, where collagen is produced.

"Because collagen is so deep within the skin, the effectiveness of commercially manufactured products which are designed for topical application is questionable," says William Daniel Keith, M.D., professor of dermatology at King-Drew Medical Center in Los Angeles, and head of the Institute for Aesthetic and Cosmetic Dermatology.

"Creams put onto the face do not penetrate into the dermis. Collagen is great if you can get it where you need it, but it is highly questionable whether or not facial cosmetics, like moisturizers which have collagen added, actually restore lasting elasticity to the skin."

Injections of collagen which plump the skin *do* penetrate into the dermis and restore elasticity. But in some black skins, hyperpigmentation or dark marks can occur.

"Collagen injections are slightly irritating to black skins. Because of the pigment, there are dark streaks where the skin has been injected. Although this hyperpigmentation can be bleached, it's a side effect which is very discouraging to some women."

ERASING WRINKLES

Chemical peel, application of a mild acid which removes the top layer of skin to reveal fresher, younger, more vibrant skin, is an effective way to erase wrinkles.

Dr. Keith recommends using a weaker strength of the peel for Black women, particularly women with darker complexions.

"It's the best way to test results and ensure that the complexion is not too light or too dark following a peel. Properly administered, the peel produces younger cells so that skin has that new glow of baby skin."

Another option is the face-lift, or *rhytidoplasty.* This cosmetic surgery tightens excess wrinkles and removes sagging skin that makes a woman look fatigued and older than she actually feels. The result is a younger, healthier, more vibrant, appearance.

There are two types of face-lifts—full and modified. The latter is a less major procedure which tightens skin at cheek and jawline. If performed before there is excessive wrinkling, the modified face-lift is quite successful.

A full face-lift involves tightening the skin at the temporal area as well. Both incision and stitches are hidden in the hairline and behind ears.

Dr. Keith recommends not waiting too long if you are considering a face-lift.

"The best result is achieved when the operation is performed before you really need it, while skin still has most of its elasticity. But on the other extreme, having a lift too early means it may have to be repeated."

THINNING HAIR

Along with age, some women face the problem of thinning hair. One solution is to wear shorter cuts layered for volume. But it takes a little wisdom to find just the right length.

Cutting hair too short means there's nothing to comb over sparse spaces. Leaving hair too long may make it appear even thinner. Styles that are a bit curlier give some hair just the body it needs.

Adding *switches,* hair extensions weaved into your own hair, can make sides, back or bangs fuller and longer. You don't have to have hair added all over, just in the sections where you want extra fullness.

This smart, easy solution also allows you to have fun with color. Try adding switches that are an interesting contrast. Best of all, only your hairdresser has to know for *sure.*

Perhaps nothing helps plump hair as effectively as does color. In addition to subtracting years by covering the gray, color coats the hair shaft so hair looks thicker, fuller, richer.

If you choose not to cover the gray, you can color to highlight the gray. It's an excellent way to brighten dull, yellowish tones, which are quite unflattering. Either way, you're sure to be satisfied with the double benefits you'll receive. Discuss your options with your hairstylist.

Minoxidil, a drug used to treat hypertension, is gaining in popularity with claims that it helps grow hair. But its use in this area is questionable. Until minoxidil is approved by the Federal Drug Administration, extreme caution is a word to the wise.

THE BEST YEARS

Sex is *better* postmenopause! Studies show that not worrying about pregnancy increases relaxation and heightens sexual enjoyment. Add to this the self-confidence that comes only with age, and it's easy to see why sexually these can be your *best* years.

Postmenopause, pelvic examinations and annual pap smears are still a must—even if one is not sexually active. Important, too, are breast self-examinations and annual mammograms.

Just as eyes, hair and body change as we get older, so do breasts. During the natural aging process women may notice their breasts become more lumpy or *fibrocystic*.

A woman should not be unduly alarmed when a physician says she has fibrocystic breasts. The doctor just means that her breasts are lumpy and difficult to examine. It does not mean that she has a greater chance or increased risk of developing breast cancer than anyone else.

Women who are fibrocystic are advised to avoid caffeine completely since it aggravates sensitivity and lumpiness. When caffeine is eliminated, breasts aren't as tender.

AND . . . ENJOY!

In addition to paying attention to all aspects of your health, take this prescription: *Enjoy!* Women today are entering new professions, continuing educational pursuits, or just relaxing. You've spent so many years working for your family's comfort. Now, reward yourself.

Is there something you've always wanted to do, but just never had the time? Now is when you have every right to be a little bit more selfish.

Learning a new sport may inspire you to exercise more, and activity-centered travel can give you a chance to meet new people, explore different lifestyles.

This is the time to remain active, to keep that body moving. And you have the wisdom that comes with years of experience, which means you have so much to offer to others.

The community needs your input, so if you're not already volunteering and have an extra hour or so daily, why not? It's an excellent way to embark on one more new adventure.

And just in case there's no one around to whisper this in your ear, let me be the one to tell you, "At your age, you're special . . . beautiful . . . just because you're *you!*"

EXTRA SENSES

Why not be as glamorous as you can, even though you're in a wheelchair? You can use the extra senses of hairstyling, cosmetics and fragrance to give the world something special to look at!

KATTIE ERRISSON

I met Kattie Errisson at a Christian retreat. Kattie, with her exuberant personality and glowing expression, usually sits on the aisle seat at the back of the small auditorium.

Whenever I passed her, I admired the pretty colors she wore, the way she styled her hair, her clean approach to makeup. But more than this, she had a warmth which emanated from her eyes and a genuine smile which always made me pause to say hello and have a brief conversation.

It was not until two years after I first met Kattie that our casual conversations blossomed into a lasting friendship. It was then that I realized she could not walk unassisted.

My initial surprise was more at her attitude than her disability. She did not *act* like a handicapped person or, rather, the way society assumes a handicapped person should act. She was Kattie, who, by the way, happened to be handicapped.

Disabled by an accident five years ago, Kattie is in rehabilitative therapy and alternates between her wheelchair and crutches. She is looking forward to being able to walk again. It was not until we took the photos for this book that Kattie told me that she used to model professionally.

Kattie believes that a lifestyle of beauty is a priority. "I don't want people to look at me and feel sorry for me. I want them to see my inner and outer radiance and say, 'She's a beautiful person.'"

But, she admits, she hasn't always felt this way.

"When I first got out of the hospital, I thought no one would pay

Photo of Kattie Errisson by George Selman. Makeup: Rudy Calvo. Hair: John Atchison

attention to me, so I did nothing to make myself look attractive. But people were looking at me! In fact, they *always* noticed me, even before my accident. So why should I expect it to be different now?"

It took time for Kattie to adjust to her new way of life, but timely encouragement provided the push she needed.

"I decided to take a dear friend's advice and come out of the doldrums. It made me feel so much better once I spent more time on my beauty treatments."

Now, with a face-framing haircut, regular skin-care treatments and just the right makeup, Kattie *really* gives people something to look at. I've asked her to share her thoughts with us.

I realize that people's abilities vary according to their disability, and you may not be able to follow all of the suggestions here. But there's a spirit, a philosophy, a special key which, I feel, will help you unlock the doors from handicapped to handicap-able.

SLIMMING HAIRCUT

Kattie's haircut is designed to frame and slim her face. The soft, short bangs which brush her forehead give her a rather playful, carefree appearance.

"This cut is so natural for me," Kattie explains. "On days when I'm rushed or just too tired from therapy, I can pull it back into a pony tail and the bangs still make me look as if I've just had my hair done."

Kattie has her hair styled professionally once a month. "Going to the salon is an investment, but when I look good I feel good and function better, so even though it's expensive, it's worth it."

Her flattering blunt cut requires minimal upkeep and the versatile length allows her to change from style to style without a lot of fuss.

To accent her features, Kattie decided to add a splash of color. "I wanted to do something different. The natural highlights from coloring my hair were a wonderful lift!"

ATTENTION-GETTING MAKEUP

Kattie's makeup is not without a motive. "I want to draw attention to my eyes," she explains. "So sometimes I wear thin, feathered eyelashes that make my own lashes look fuller and thicker. Lining underneath my bottom lashes makes my eyes sparkle."

To give her eyes depth, she uses rich brown earth tones. On her yellowundertoned complexion, burnt-orange cheek and lip color warm her skin.

"I wanted to see how best to apply colors, so a professional makeup session was my therapeutic splurge. Now that I know the basics, experimenting with different looks is exciting."

EXERCISE EVERY DAY

"Exercise is more important than makeup, hair—all of that," says Kattie. "It makes me feel better about myself, and I tell myself that I *am* better for exercising. To me, there's no substitute for eating well and doing all I can do to stay healthy."

Working with her therapist, Kattie is concentrating on strengthening her leg muscles. "But I listen to my body and only work at a pace that's comfortable for me."

THE EXTRAS

Kattie explains that these extras are equally important to her beauty regimen.

"I love jewelry, but I feel it's important to accessorize tastefully so that the attention is on me and not on my jewelry. I wear lots of perfume, not to be fragrant for others, but for me," says Kattie.

"And, I go to the dentist and see my eye doctor regularly, especially since I'm approaching forty."

Not to be overlooked is Kattie's positive mental attitude, which is what really makes her as beautiful as she is.

"I have so much to be thankful for. It's easy to concentrate on the negatives, to focus on what is lacking. But I'd rather challenge myself and shift my energies to the larger side of the scale. That's where the blessings far outweigh any disability!"

Kattie is realistic about the challenge ahead of her, and although it's not exactly fun, every success is rewarding. As she focuses efforts to walk again, giving up is not in her vocabulary.

Whatever *you* do, don't give up!

SENSUALITY

Sensuality involves who you are as a total woman. It encompasses your body, your mind, your spirit. Knowing yourself and liking yourself are essential to express your femininity.

A woman who genuinely feels good about herself feels good to be around. Because she thoughtfully, consistently cares for herself, she demonstrates an admirable level of self-esteem. In turn, she reinforces her sense of self-worth and contributes to that healthy, positive attitude most men find irresistible!

SELF-IMAGE

According to the renowned Alvin Poussaint, M.D., associate professor of psychiatry and associate dean of the Harvard Medical School, "Men are still attracted to the attractive. A woman who invests time in health and beauty regimens fosters her own self-image and is more likely to establish good relationships. In developing herself, she becomes more and more secure with who she is, and she is often more trusting, more positive and less defensive with others."

This, he explains, is in contrast with the woman whose self-esteem totters. "A woman who does not like herself may not invest time in improving her appearance and she may unwittingly project a negative self-image to the detriment of her own popularity. In a sense, her sexuality suffers."

Dr. Poussaint feels that, in general, today's Black woman has a positive perception. "She has a new respect for her own beauty. She has a certain personal standard, and, above all, she is secure enough with her ethnicity to be creative in developing her own style."

AN ATTRACTIVE REACTION

Looking attractive and having people react to you because you are attractive is an important aspect which increases self-esteem and is an adjunct to healthy sexuality.

"Of course, qualities of character and personality are equally important," says Dr. Poussaint. "But initially, men are attracted to women who care about their figure, wear fashionable hairstyles and apply cosmetics smartly."

Since there will always be other women who are more attractive, Dr. Poussaint feels it's important to avoid comparisons.

"Women who make a practice of comparing themselves with others never feel stunning. Part of the need to compare is related to low self-esteem. The question every woman needs to ask herself is who becomes her ideal and upon what criteria are these standards based?"

The paradox of women who *are* attractive yet *feel* unattractive may have more to do with what they think about themselves *inside* rather than how they look *outside.*

"Physical attraction is a thin façade if inside a woman doesn't feel good about herself. It's especially evident in the very attractive woman who lives in an unattractive manner," says Dr. Poussaint. "Her home, for example, may remain in a state of disarray. Although she presents an acceptable image outwardly, her environment indicates that inwardly she feels just like her surroundings."

Beauty, he insists, has to be more than just skin-deep. Self-esteem, the awareness of who you really are, is essential to beauty.

SELF-ESTEEM

"Self-esteem involves objective introspection," advises Minnie Claiborne, Ph.D., a psychologist and Christian counselor practicing in Mobile, Alabama.

In her self-esteem seminars she suggests, "Evaluate your best assets and magnify these. Don't focus on your weaker points."

Dr. Claiborne suggests we draw mental pictures of how we are when we're at our best and remind ourselves daily of these talents and abilities which make us so special.

"Itemizing your talents is similar to seeing makeup colors applied step by step. When you see each individual color, you can truly appreciate the finished product."

This principle, says Dr. Claiborne, works the same in isolating individual attributes.

Photo: George Barkentin. Courtesy Vogue Beauty Book. *Copyright © 1981/2 Condé Nast Publications, Inc.*

"When you can isolate your personal assets, even making a list of them, you're not likely to measure yourself and come up short. During periods of stress, instead of having a pity party, you will be better equipped to reinforce self-esteem by telling yourself the truth about who you are."

Spending time with the right people is an important aspect of self-esteem. Dr. Claiborne notes that overweight women who only socialize with women who are also overweight subconsciously choose comfortable mirrors of themselves. Absent is the incentive to change, the challenge to action. Instead, negative images feed off each other.

"You may have to limit your friends to spend more time with people who better express who you really are. It's also necessary to reevaluate your relationship with people who are critical of you. So-called friends who use teasing or joking as a way of making negative comments chip away rather than build self-esteem."

On the other hand, the ability to accept compliments graciously, is a positive expression of self-esteem.

"A woman can enter a room and be so captivating that everyone notices her. But how does she perceive herself? When she is complimented, does she say 'Thank you,' or does she begin to point out that her dress is not new or that she has a pimple?"

Dr. Claiborne reminds us not to magnify such imperfections. "You know when you look attractive. You've invested time and money to put your best face forward. Why minimize your beauty by putting yourself down?"

And although some women measure their self-worth by the presence of a relationship, this yardstick, she says, is unreliable.

"The love songs are not true! You *are* whole and complete without him. You *can* live without him. Yes, a relationship is wonderful, but your self-esteem should not be contingent upon whether or not it exists. He may not realize how valuable you are, and that's unfortunate for him. What's really important when you close the door is that *you* understand *your* worth. Don't crumble. Remind yourself of how incredible and precious you really are."

As a final suggestion, Dr. Claiborne echoes the same advice you probably heard as a child.

"Hold your head up! Sit up straight! Walk tall! The person *inside* will stretch to the full measure of self-esteem you express *outside.*"

A Closing Note

THERE'S MORE TO BEAUTY

"Be beautiful inside, in your hearts,
with the lasting charm of a gentle and
quiet spirit which is so precious to God."
I Peter 3:4 (The Living Bible)

Yes, there's more to beauty than what meets the eye. Who you are inside defines what you are like on the outside. The key to *outer* beauty is *inner* beauty.

Qualities which can be sensed rather than seen are what count most. This gentle, quiet beauty cannot be purchased in a bottle or put on with a brush. It's timeless . . . priceless . . . and it comes from the Spirit.

Gratitude is an essential quality. It treasures life's little gifts, the ones we usually take for granted. The opposite of gratitude is jealousy, an emotion that wastes precious time because it's busy thinking that what everyone else has is better.

Anger is a beauty robber. Like an invisible barrier, it dispels others. The roots of anger go deep, and its causes can be varied. Honestly expressing yourself when you are upset is admirable. But uncontrolled outbursts make even the prettiest woman seem unattractive. Sometimes it takes professional help to unmask the hurt inside, but the rewards are well worth the effort.

Perhaps nothing is more refreshing than a warm sense of humor. Even in a crisis, the woman who can smile instead of criticize or complain is endearing. Being hard on others—and yourself—forces you to be judgmental. Life easily becomes a courtroom where you sentence people to the prison of your mind.

Trust and vulnerability are the tender sides of beauty. Sincerity, graciousness and generosity are beauty's natural expressions. Loyalty and dependability are what make beauty precious.

Photo of Vivian Ford by George Selman

Forgiveness—of others and of yourself—will make you feel lighter than any crash diet.

And what your grandmother told you when you were a child is still true. A personal relationship with God through Jesus Christ is the inner expression of a love experience.

REFERENCES

NUTRITION

George Berkley. *On Being Black and Healthy—How Black Americans Can Lead Longer and Healthier Lives.* Englewood Cliffs, N.J.: Prentice-Hall, 1982.

Jane Brody. *Jane Brody's Nutrition Book: A Lifetime Guide to Good Eating for Better Health and Weight Control.* New York: W. W. Norton & Company, 1981.

———. *The New York Times Guide to Personal Health.* New York: Times Books, 1982.

Benjamin Colimore, and Sarah Stewart. *Nutrition and Your Body* (rev. ed.). Los Angeles: Light Wave Press, 1974.

M. S. Franz, R.D., and J. Marion. "Fast Food—Where's the Nutrition?," *Diabetes Forecast,* November 1985.

William Kannel, M.D., Joseph T. Doyle, M.D., et al., "Optimal Resources for Primary Prevention of Atherosclerotic Diseases," *Report of Inter-Society Commission for Heart Disease Resources,* Vol. 70, July 1984.

Saul Kent. "How Dietary Salt Contributes to Hypertension," *Geriatrics,* Vol. 36, No. 6, June 1981.

Jean A. T. Pennington and Helen Nichols Church. *Bowes and Church's Food Values of Portions Commonly Used* (13th ed.). New York: Harper & Row, 1980.

Claude C. Roy, M.D., and Narmer Galeano, M.D. "Childhood Antecedents of Adult Degenerative Disease," *Pediatric Clinics of North America,* Vol. 32, No. 2, April 1985.

HAIR CARE

Gerald A. Spencer, M.D. *Cosmetology in the Negro: A Guide to Its Problems.* New York: Arlain Printing Company, 1944.

————. *Your Hair and You.* New York: Milady Publishing Corp., 1957.

SKIN CARE

Charles McDonald, M.D. Chapter 64, "Dermatology of Black Skin," in *Practice of Medicine,* Vol. 1, Hagerstown, Md.: Harper & Row, 1977.

Humbert Pierantoni. *Essential Notions About Black Skin.* Paris: Editions Les Nouvelles Esthétiques, 1952.

POSTURE

Wilfred Barlow. *The Alexander Technique.* New York: Alfred A. Knopf, 1973.

Index